No Regrets
Things I Learned
at My Mother's Knee
and Other Joints

Bonnie Hutchinson

Dear Mavis,
Hope you enjoy
stories from our
Parents' generation!
Best wishes,
Bonnie

Transformation
Publishing

Edmonton Alberta

For information about permission to reproduce selections from this
book, please contact
Permissions
Transformation Publishing
#720, 11007 Jasper Avenue NW
Edmonton Alberta T5K 0K6 Canada
Bonnie@BonnieHutchinson.com

Cover design by Ian Kirkpatrick, iankirkpatrick@shaw.ca
Cover photo courtesy of Alberta Order of Excellence
Author photo by Stephanie Cragg, steph99@telus.net
Production by Budget Printing Edmonton, https://bprint.com/

Thanks to Dr. Roger Epp and University of Alberta Press for
permission to include "Dr. Fowler," a prose poem by Dr. Roger Epp
in *Only Leave a Trace: Meditations*,
Edmonton: University of Alberta Press, 2017, p. 36.

ISBN 978 099 210 8618

Transformation Publishing
#720, 11007 Jasper Avenue NW, Edmonton Alberta T5K 0K6 Canada
www.BonnieHutchinson.com

Dedicated to
Blain Fowler and Beth Balshaw
and in memory of Bruce Fowler,
with thanks for sharing childhoods,

and to the spirits of our parents
Bill Fowler and Berdie Fowler
who shaped us, supported us and
released us to become what we became

Contents

Prelude

No Regrets

May 1991: About two weeks before our parents'
Fifty-first wedding anniversary

Dad danced at a wedding on Saturday night, flipped pancakes at a fly-in breakfast Sunday morning and debated at a political event Monday afternoon. Tuesday he attended meetings and that evening presented an award at the year-end Air Cadet parade. He met Mom for coffee at a hotel café and told her he was proud of her for something that happened that day. (Mom didn't tell us what the "something" was.)

On the way to their respective cars, Dad saw some Air Cadet buddies in the lounge and decided to join them. Mom carried on home. His parting words were, "See you in a bit."

Not much later, Dad had some kind of collapse in the lounge. He told his buddies, "I think you better take me to the hospital." They walked him to his car, laid him in the back seat and drove him to the hospital.

From the hospital, the Air Cadet buddies called my brother. He phoned Mom from the hospital, told her Dad was in Emergency, and went to pick her up. By the time Mom arrived at the hospital, Dad was gone.

On that terrible night for our family, back at Mom's home trying to grasp that our dad was dead, my mother said this:

"You know, I have no regrets. We did all the things we wanted to do together, and we said all the things we wanted to say to each other."

I thought, what an amazing thing to be able to say. "No regrets." What a comfort. And I knew that if I were to die right then, I would not be able to say I had no regrets.

I resolved to change that.

Dr. Fowler

In 2008, University of Alberta Augustana Campus awarded our mom, Berdie Fowler, an Honourary Doctorate of Laws.

Dr. Roger Epp, who in 2008 was Dean of Augustana Campus, wrote this…

She has brokered no peace, discovered no cures, written nothing that should win a Nobel Prize. She had no degree to her name, in fact, until the afternoon when she was dressed in ceremonial robes and hooded in front of the Class of 2008. She was born in a farmhouse, not far away, in 1920. She has lived in the same small city most of her adult life. Her nomination must have raised some eyebrows when it came; for surely it will bring the university no global lustre.

In the streets where she is known by name, though, where her first name is enough, she is the pre-eminent citizen, a woman ahead of her time, and never for herself alone. She is the champion of learning and public service. She is the voice of reason in the Tuesday paper – sometimes protective, sometimes bold, always clear.

At the podium, Doctor Fowler takes only a few well-timed minutes to earn her degree with words as artful and dignified as her long life. On this afternoon, the university has got it right.

~ Roger Epp, *Only Leave a Trace: Meditations*
(Edmonton: University of Alberta Press, 2017), p. 36.
Reprinted by permission.

Nobody grows up in the same family

Once, as adults, my sister Beth and I had a conversation in which I learned to my amazement that she grew up knowing she was loved no matter what. I grew up believing that love was always conditional, depending on if I obeyed the rules, measured up and did the right thing.

At various moments during that conversation, the expressions on both our faces asked, "How could you think that?" Of course, we were both right. As Beth said, "Nobody grows up in the same family as anyone else."

As I began writing this, I debated whether to ask my brother Blain and sister Beth, our children and grandchildren and the children of our brother Bruce who has died, what they learned from the woman who was our mother and grandmother.

I decided not to ask any of them. This book summarizes some of what I learned growing up as Berdie Fowler's daughter. Others of her descendants learned different things.

I know she would be delighted by some of what I learned. I also know she would be appalled or mystified by some of my interpretations of what I learned.

This book was first conceived about 4 a.m. one night in Mexico, when I was awakened with the phrase: "Things I learned at my mother's knee and other joints." It was about three months after Mom died and I could feel her enjoying the words. I was compelled to go out onto the balcony and, in the moonlight, began to "transcribe" chapter headings.

My wish for you as you read this is that, not only will you resonate with some things I learned, but you'll reflect on what you learned at your mother's knee and other joints, and consider whether what you learned then is true for you now.

Symphony

Be clear

I have no childhood memories of wondering what my mom expected of me. I was always clear because she was always clear. I didn't always live up to her expectations but I knew what they were.

In the last years of Mom's life, her clarity was a gift to our family.

~~~~~

She was in her early eighties when she had her first serious heart incident. A few years later, in hospital after another heart episode, Mom's condition was serious enough that her heart monitor was at the nursing station. On a Sunday morning, her heart stopped. This triggered a flurry of staff rushing to her room. And then her heart started again. Nobody knew why it stopped. Nobody knew why it started again. One of the nurses said, "It just rebooted."

That afternoon, four or five family members from different branches of her descendants were visiting her. As she sat propped up in her hospital bed, she said, "While you're all here…"

She had our attention.

She looked around the room at us and said. "I've known many people who have now died." Then she used the phrase that meant, "Listen up!" She said, "It's been my observation…" We were definitely paying attention.

"I've known many people who have now died. It's been my observation that sometimes in the last few months of their lives, some people have had different kinds of medical procedures. It often seemed to me they experienced a great deal of unnecessary pain and discomfort because of that. They might have been better off to let nature take its course."

She looked around again.

She explained that she had a Personal Directive, a document which stated her wishes if for some reason she was not able to make decisions on her own behalf. She had just learned that her Personal Directive did not accomplish what she intended.

"Jim will be coming here tomorrow morning to look after that," she said. Jim was her lawyer. In her home community, her lawyer would indeed visit her in hospital and ensure proper legal documents were in place.

"In the meantime," she said (meaning, "In case I die before morning"), "I want you to know some things." She looked at each of us again.

"I have no fear of death," she said. "I've thought I was dying a few times, and it's not scary at all. I've lived a wonderful life and as far as I know I'm on good terms with everyone. Death holds no fear for me."

I took that in for future reference in my life.

"If there comes a time when I can't make decisions for myself, I don't want heroic measures to keep me alive. I'm ready to go. But while I'm alive, I would like no pain if possible. I want as little discomfort as possible. I want to be comfortable."

She paused. "And," she said and smiled at each of us, "I'd like to be beautiful."

Got it.

We were clear. She knew and we knew that, with several branches of her children and grandchildren in the room, we all understood her wishes and would act accordingly.

~~~~~

A few weeks later, my brother, sister and I all received letters in Mom's lovely cursive handwriting, expressing her confidence that we knew her wishes. She stated that my brother would be the first person authorized to make decisions on her behalf because he lived in her community. If he were not available, I would be the second person because I lived the next closest, and our sister would be the third person because she lived further away.

Mom stressed that the order of authority had only to do with practicalities and was not a reflection on any of us. She attached a copy of the Personal Directive she had worked out with her lawyer.

~~~~~

As children, we knew what Mom expected of us. As adults we did too. In the years after Dad died, her clarity continued. It eliminated a lot of dithering, wondering what was the right thing to do.

For example…

For several years after Dad died, we still gathered at Mom's house for Christmas dinner. By then, our family of her children, grandchildren and great-grandchildren had grown to more than two dozen people. Her Calgary family usually stayed with her for a day or two over the holidays. Though we all tried to help, even just the organizing of Christmas dinner was a big production, especially considering that Mom was still working full time at the family paper.

Then one November we received a fax from Mom, ,typewritten and double spaced. The message said, "I would like to have Christmas dinner with the whole family, but not on Christmas day and not at my house. I propose we meet for dinner at a restaurant. I'll buy. Here are possible dates…"

Crystal clear.

Be clear

~~~~~

When Mom moved out of her home and into a seniors' lodge, she said, "I'm ready to make this move, but I'm not ready to sell the house yet." Absolutely clear.

After that, when out-of-town children or grandchildren came to visit, they would stay at her house and Mom would join them.

And then one day, she said, "Okay, I'm ready to list the house for sale."

~~~~~

When Mom's house was sold and possessions needed to be removed, Mom had cracked a rib and was in extreme pain. Clearly she would not be able to do much in the way of preparing the home for new owners.

Mom phoned each of her children and adult grandchildren to explain how she wanted to dispose of the contents. She said, "I'd like you to go to the house sometime in the next ten days. On the table in the family room is a sheet of foolscap. Walk through the house and decide what you'd like to have. Write it on the sheet of paper. If nobody else wants it, it's yours. If somebody else wants it, I'll draw names to decide who gets it."

Done!

And, despite being in great pain, she was able to direct proceedings – clearly! – about what would go where as the house was prepared for new owners.

~~~~~

In the last few days of Mom's life (and we knew it was her last few days), at one point her doctor recommended that she have a blood transfusion. My brother and I were both present and of course we knew her wishes for no discomfort. The doctor thought the blood transfusion would enable her to be more comfortable. We were not sure.

The hospital staff got ready for the transfusion and waited for us to give the go-ahead. We agonized for a bit and then decided that, if the doctor thought it would help her be more comfortable, maybe it was okay to go ahead. The hospital staff prepared to insert a needle into Mom's arm for the transfusion.

By now, Mom was asleep most of the time, and very weak when she was somewhat awake. As my brother and I were in the hallway, my daughter, who'd been in Mom's room, came out and said, "Grandma is saying, 'Don't, don't, don't.'" Mom's voice was so weak it was barely audible, but her wishes were clear.

End of procedure.

I was so grateful that both my brother and I had come to the same (incorrect) conclusion – so no possibility of "I told you so." Most of all, I am forever grateful that even in her barely there condition as her body was shutting down, Mom was still being clear and still in charge of her life.

~~~~~

A postscript.

After Mom died, cleaning out her room at the lodge, in her desk I found a page in her handwriting entitled, "When I die."

She began, "At some point I will die. I don't believe in leaving funeral instructions, because I don't know what the circumstances will be. However…"

She then mentioned the name of a person she hoped could officiate if he was available (he was). She listed her favourite Bible verse as a child; a favourite hymn; and her most common prayer: "Gratitude, and 'Thy will be done.'" She especially hoped someone would say how grateful she and Dad were for the many ways the community supported them in the years they struggled to launch their fledging weekly paper.

Yep, still being clear.

Be gracious

It was Christmas Eve in the year I'd left my husband, and the year after our dad died. I was staying overnight at Mom's home. In contrast to earlier years when lots of family would have gathered at my parents' home on Christmas Eve, there were just the two of us. We were settling into a quiet evening, doing a few things to prepare for the next day's big family Christmas dinner, watching some Christmas things on TV.

The doorbell rang. We looked at each other in curiosity. Who could it be?

Mom went to the door. I could hear the voice. It was the husband I'd left earlier in the year. My heart started to pound. I did not want to be in the same room with him.

Mom was gracious as always. She said pleasant things, thanked him for the card he gave her and then said, "Would you like to come in?"

I was thinking, "No, no, no!"

And then I heard her say, graciously, "...or, do you have other places you need to be?" I heard him say something and I heard her close the door and lock it.

She returned and said, "Well, that worked out well, didn't it? We both knew our lines." And she grinned wickedly.

~~~~~

Mom told us she was shy as a little girl. She didn't like meeting new people. She didn't like being in crowds. She didn't like having to speak to others, especially people she didn't know.

Mom didn't begin school until she was seven, waiting a year so she and her younger sister Edna could start school together. Mom and Edna rode a pony to Ellswick School, a one-room rural schoolhouse whose lone teacher somehow managed to teach all subjects, Grades One to Eight, for the children who lived in the farming district.

The big kids helped the little kids. All students had to do a lot of work on their own as the teacher gave assignments and taught other grades. Mom said there were advantages to hearing the work of other grades while they worked on their own. By the time they got to Grade Six arithmetic, for example, they'd been hearing snippets of it for five years.

At the end of Grade Eight, most students were done with school but Mom's and Edna's parents – unusual for the era – thought they should go on to high school. To do that, at ages 15 and 14, Mom and Edna had to leave their farm home and move to Camrose.

Back in the one-room schoolhouse they knew everyone and everyone's family. In the "huge" community of Camrose (population a few thousand – overwhelming!), more students were in one classroom than had been in their entire rural school. They didn't know anyone. It was noisy. It was crowded. Instead of one teacher there were several, all with different styles.

Mom was homesick and miserable. She decided she just couldn't do it. It was too hard.

At Canadian Thanksgiving in early October, Mom and Edna went home to the farm for the weekend. Mom told her mother that she was never going back. It was just too hard.

Her mother was completely unsympathetic. "I never had the chance to go to school, and you do," her mother said. "You are *not* quitting." And that was that.

Mom had to figure out how to cope.

~~~~~

Gradually she noticed that some other students might be almost as shy and frightened and uncomfortable as she was.

Gradually she began to say "Hello" to a few people. Gradually she figured out that one way to ease her shyness – at least a little – was to ask people something about themselves.

And that, she discovered, was magic.

~~~~~

As a child and then a teenager, I was always surprised to hear my mom talk about once being shy and uncomfortable. By the time I was old enough to notice, to me she always seemed sure of herself. She was never loud or noticeably outgoing, just confident. As I watched and listened, I gradually pieced together that she learned to be comfortable in groups because she stopped focusing on herself and focused on other people.

I watched during a Christmas gathering with friends on our street. As a kid, I'd heard Mom and her friend talking about the friend's mother-in-law who would be visiting from out of town. The mother-in-law was known to be cranky and critical of my mom's friend.

At the gathering, I watched my mom go up to the mother-in- law and ask some friendly innocuous question. In almost no time, the mother-in-law was chatting away happily and actually smiled.

Another time I listened as Mom told Dad about her evening as a guest speaker in a smaller community. Before the formal part of the evening began, Mom made a point of asking people about things she'd noticed in their community. Then, during her talk, she told them how impressed she was. The most important thing was, she was genuinely interested and genuinely impressed.

"People like to be noticed," she said.

~~~~~

Over the years, I watched and listened as Mom visited family and friends, directed staff, chatted to people in grocery store line-ups, chaired meetings, listened to a World War II veteran tell some of his horrors in wartime Europe. I watched and listened to her admire the treasured family photos of residents in a care facility, give presentations, listen to her great grandchildren read…

She was unfailingly courteous, unfailingly gracious. She appeared to give each person her undivided attention. It seemed to me that most people felt better after they spent time with her.

(In private, I sometimes had other experiences, but that's a different chapter!)

~~~~~

So how did that shy farm girl morph into this gracious woman who was good in groups and comfortable in leadership positions?

Sometime when she was in her mid-eighties, Mom summed up the journey.

"When you're young," she said, "You worry about what people think about you. When you're middle aged, you don't worry so much about what people think of you."

Then she laughed. "When you get old," she said, "You find out nobody was thinking about you anyway!"

Be your own person

"So did you kill him?"

Those were the opening words of a phone call to my mom, from one of her friends who'd been at an early morning meeting that both my parents attended.

At the meeting, Mom put forward a motion. Dad argued against Mom's motion and voted against it.

Mom's friend thought Mom would be furious. Mom thought it was funny.

Whatever else she might have expected from our dad, him agreeing with her opinions was not one of her expectations.

During election times, I'd listen to my parents disagree on who they would vote for and why. Many election evenings, they'd have conversation like, "So, did we cancel out each other's votes again?" and then they'd laugh.

A great lesson for me as a kid: that people could have different opinions without animosity. They could have different opinions and still love each other and like each other.

~~~~~

Mom grew up in a generation in which it was expected that women would be financially supported by a man. Women's work was to run the household, care for children and cater to their husbands. Men's work was to support the family and interact with the outside world.

In Mom's generation, women were often addressed by their husband's names: "Mrs. Bill Fowler." It's like women had no identity of their own but were defined by their husbands. For example, the wives of two brothers were known as "Mrs. Dave" and "Mrs. Gord."

In my early twenties, I remember once thinking, as I considered my own life and looked around at other young women I knew, that women's lives were completely dependent on who they married. They would be financially comfortable or poor, live in a beautiful home or a hovel, be treated respectfully or not, all depending on their husband.

Women who had no husband were pitied. Too bad no man wanted them. Women whose husbands had died received sympathy now that they had no man to look after them. On forms asking for one's occupation (yes, occupation not marital status), "Widow" was often listed as an occupation.

So, as a young woman in my twenties with two small children, I was surprised when one day Mom said, "Doesn't matter who you are, married or single, male or female, everybody has to learn to look after themselves." It was fine if somebody was around to look after you, but it was important to be capable of looking after yourself if it should become necessary.

Radical thinking for someone of her generation. At that time, it was radical thinking even for *my* generation.

How did she get there?

~~~~~

Maybe it began when she had to leave her farm home at age 15 in order to go to high school in the "huge" town of Camrose. Nowadays it would be a 20-minute drive from the farm to Camrose. Then it would be a half-day journey – *if* you could get through the muddy quarter mile near Roper's Store. Commuting was out of the question. Essentially, she had to be an adult from that point on.

Maybe it was when she got her first job as secretary to Chester Ronning, the principal of Camrose Lutheran College where she attended post-high-school business college. She thought Chester Ronning was a wise and important man and she took great pride in being good at her job.

Maybe it was shortly after she and Dad were married and there was a war on in Europe. He enlisted in the Royal Canadian Air Force and was posted to many places across Canada.

Rather than go home to her parents as many military wives did, Mom travelled with Dad for several years until he was posted overseas. As they moved from place to place across Canada, meeting new people everywhere they went, he often went on to the new posting while she had to stay for a while, handling everything on her own, with one and then two small children.

She once told me about the days after I was born in Regina, where Dad happened to be posted. Dad was there on the day I was born, but soon after he had to leave to his new posting in Ontario.

In those days, new moms were in hospital for a week or ten days. When she got out of hospital with her brand new first baby, she had to pack up and travel by train by herself to Dad's new location – a distance of about 2,700 km (1,700 miles)..

Scary! But she did it.

Perhaps there's something to be said for "no choice."

~~~~~

After the war, when Dad returned from overseas and our family grew to two adults and four children, Mom continued to play a traditional role. But when the *Booster* launched, she was fully involved in the business. She wasn't trying to forge a new role for women. She was just doing what had to be done to support her husband and the family.

From that springboard of being actively involved in the business – and a business whose customers were mostly other businesses – Mom continued to do things that most women in that era did not do.

As well, she was no longer just "Mrs. Bill Fowler." She began to have an identity of her own. She assumed leadership positions in various community organizations. Later, she was appointed to some provincial boards and committees.

It seemed to me that the most telling "be your own person" time came when Dad retired from the *Booster*.

Dad retired but Mom did not.

Wow.

~~~~~

Mom insisted that Dad <u>not</u> just lounge around home (and probably pout). She insisted that he continue to go out every day and meet her for coffee at 9:30 a.m. and 3:30 p.m. She also went home for lunch with him most days.

Dad continued with his numerous community activities. (When did he have time to work before that?) Mom continued her role at the *Booster*, along with various community activities that did not involve him.

She clearly established a life and identity of her own, separate from his life and identity.

That served her well after Dad died. We all knew there was not a day in her life when she didn't think of him and miss him. After she moved into an assisted living facility, when she opened her eyes in the morning, the first thing she saw was his carefully placed photo. She often told fond stories about him.

But she had her own identity.

She was her own person, capable and in charge of her life.

As a young woman and then an adult observing her, I did not miss that lesson.

Do what needs to be done

Late in her life, Mom commented one day, "You know, all the things I've done were nothing like what I thought I would be doing or what I would have chosen."

~~~~~

As a teenager, after working part time at the local hospital, Mom wanted more than anything else to learn how to be a nurse and go to Africa to help people there.

Her mom was not impressed. "Why do you want to go to Africa? Couldn't you help people right here?"

Her father ended the conversation. At that time in that community, most teenagers, male or female, as soon as they turned 15 or finished Grade Eight, dropped out of school to work on the family farm or at a job in town.

In response to the idea of my mom training to be a nurse, her father pointed out that, since she had finished Grade Twelve AND taken an additional year of business college, he had already paid for more education than most girls could ever expect.

End of conversation.

~~~~~

The year of business school after high school was pivotal. That was the year she learned bookkeeping and typing and other skills that became central to her work for the weekly paper she and my dad later launched.

Business College was also the year she and our dad became an item. She went to work as a stenographer in the office of Chester Ronning, the principal of Camrose Lutheran College where she'd taken the business course. She what needed to be done and continued to do so after she and Dad were married.

~~~~~

I didn't realize what I was learning as our family circumstances changed.

In those days, "housewife" was considered a full time occupation. Few married women worked outside their home.

When my Dad and Grandpa had a falling out, we left the upstairs suite in Mom's parents' home and moved to a new home in the "West End" of Camrose (now considered part of City Centre).

My parents couldn't afford a refrigerator. For a few years, we kept milk in pails of cool water in the basement. My parents also couldn't afford a washer and dryer. They did manage to acquire an olden-days wringer washer. For years, Mom hung the damp clothes on clotheslines strung up in the basement.

I don't recall her ever complaining about any of that. She just did what needed to be done.

As an adult, observing my mother's prudence and my father's enjoyment of some degree of risk, I've always assumed it was Dad's choice to launch the *Camrose Booster* and Mom agreed to go along with it.

She set up a card table in their bedroom to do the typing and artwork and bookkeeping that the paper required. As the *Booster* was still finding its feet, she also got a job at the local Variety Store to help bring in some income. And of course, she continued to do all the "housewife" tasks that two adults and four kids required. She did what needed to be done.

I do remember her once saying, in a voice louder than usual, "I'm doing three full time jobs!"

~~~~~

That "do what needs to be done" approach extended beyond the family. When the local association for children with developmental disabilities was trying to build a special school, Mom was on the fundraising committee.

When I was a young single mom struggling to find reliable affordable child care for my two pre-school children, Mom was chair of a local committee to create the first children's daycare centre in rural Alberta. (The daycare centre opened the year my youngest child started school.)

When, at Dad's urging, Mom joined him as a member of the local Chamber of Commerce, after a few years she agreed to be on the executive. Later, when she was asked to serve as President, she said "yes," becoming the first woman in Alberta and only the second woman in Canada to hold such office.

When the local College was fundraising for a proper library, Mom was part of the campaign.

Back at the *Booster* office, as technology changed, Mom was overseeing changes in how pages were produced (no more pen and ink on metal plates!) and how accounting was managed (electronically, not in a manual ledger). She learned what she had to learn and did what had to be done.

~~~~~

That "do what needs to be done" mentality was part of Mom's character but it also grew out of the years when she was growing up. On the prairies, everyone in her generation grew up in the Great Depression. They lived through hardships I can't even imagine, and did what needed to be done to survive. Then as the Depression was easing came World War II. Most young men went off to war. They too were doing what they believed needed to be done.

Many years later, one evening when I was visiting Mom overnight, she was being especially judgmental of "young people" who seemed to be unhappy and lacking in direction or motivation. Since the category of "young people" included my young adult children, I was feeling defensive on their behalf. I was also irritated at her "implacable rightness."

But I thought about it overnight.

In the morning, I asked her, "So, is it bothering you that young people seem so unhappy when you remember that at about their age you were living through the Depression, and then seeing your husband go off to war and not knowing if you'd ever see him again?"

'Yes!" she said. "I don't understand why young people today are so worried and unhappy. They're safe. They're looked after. They have nothing to be frightened of."

~~~~~

On the day Mom commented, "You know, all the things I've done were nothing like what I thought I would be doing or what I would have chosen," I asked her, "What would you have chosen?"

That was when she told me the story of once wishing she could be a nurse. She said that as she grew older, she would have loved to learn more about psychology and sociology.

Then she added that, over the years, what she really wished was that she could start some kind of program for people who, for whatever reason, found it hard to get on in the world. She imagined a setting where they could do meaningful work, and have friends and community. They would also have some parts of their lives – the parts they really couldn't manage – looked after in some respectful way.

I knew she was thinking of specific individuals.

I thought of her career in business – which began because she was doing what needed to be done to support her husband and family.

I thought of some of her community activities over the years – doing what needed to be done for sub-sets of people in Camrose and district.

I thought of her appointments to several provincial bodies – doing what needed to be done, especially related to business and her industry in our province.

~~~~~

In the entryway of a care facility I drive by often, a sign says, "Bloom where you're planted."

I think that's what Mom did.

Earn your place

"I knew I'd been accepted when they stopped being nice to me," she said.

Mom was a pathfinder in many ways, but "pathfinder" was never her motivation. It was a by-product of doing what she thought needed to be done.

Her statement about being accepted was referring to the Alberta Opportunity Company. I'll get to that in a minute.

~~~~~

Mom was uncomfortable with the term "feminist." She preferred "humanist." But there's no doubt she observed and resented some of the ways in which women in her generation were treated "less than."

On one occasion, after she had finished negotiating a large financial transaction, she noted with satisfaction that, not only was she a female client, but the bank representative was also female. Every aspect of the transaction had been handled by a woman. That pleased her.

She may have been reacting to an experience I'd had when I applied for a mortgage. I'd been head of a household for more than five years and met all the financial requirements in terms of income, cash flow, secure employment and credit rating. Even so, the bank wanted one more thing: a male co-signer like my dad or (even more insulting!) my younger brother.

Mom did activities that contributed to the advancement of women's place in society, but it bothered her when a woman on one of her committees made a production out of who made the coffee. It's not that Mom didn't get the point. It's that she thought the tactic generated irritation and therefore resistance. Making a big deal out of who made the coffee was counter-productive to the bigger picture.

Her style was different. She thought if you just quietly went about doing a good job, the resistance would gradually evaporate.

When she was elected President of the local Chamber of Commerce – the first woman in Alberta and the second woman in Canada to hold that position – several men resigned. They felt a woman had no business holding that position.

Mom was keenly aware of the opposition. She just didn't acknowledge it. She went about doing an excellent job and assumed that eventually the members would return. They did.

~~~~~

Speaking of "women's place," one story was the source of enormous hilarity in our family.

One day at the *Booster* front counter, Mom was dealing with a man who, quite belligerently, wanted the *Booster* to do something it would not do.

Finally in frustration, the man said, "Let me talk to your manager!"

Mom rose to her full five foot eight and said, quietly and politely of course, "I am the manager."

The idea of anyone challenging Mom's authority seemed incredibly funny to her family.

~~~~~

That brings us to the Alberta Opportunity Company.

The Alberta Opportunity Company (AOC) was an Alberta Crown Corporation founded in 1972. Its independent board of directors reported directly to the Alberta legislature through the Minister of Economic Development and Trade.

AOC provided financial and management assistance to qualified small- and medium-sized Alberta businesses that were not able to obtain reasonable terms and conditions from regular banks.

The provincial government invited Mom to serve on the AOC board, and she accepted. She was the first woman ever appointed to that board.

Just as when she became President of the local Chamber of Commerce, she knew there was opposition to her appointment. One of those opposed was the Chair of the Board.

As was her style, she did not acknowledge the opposition. She just quietly went about being a competent credible board member.

~~~~~

As part of the Alberta Opportunity Company, board members would fly to different locations in Alberta and meet all day with a break for lunch at a local restaurant.

When the meetings were in Edmonton or Calgary (places to which Mom would drive), Dad sometimes came along. He would do other things while Mom was at the meeting, and often join the group for lunch. Mom was, of course, still the only woman in the group.

Then came the day – one of the days when Dad had joined the group for lunch – when the all-day meeting was held in a boardroom at an exclusive private club. When the group broke for lunch and went into the dining room for lunch, the Maitre D' stopped Mom at the door. "I'm sorry, Madam," he said. "You are not allowed to come in. This is a men-only dining room."

What?

Clearly nobody had been aware of this policy when the boardroom was booked and lunch reservations arranged.

Different men in the group had different expressions on their faces – some surprised, some outraged, some incredulous, some just uncomfortable.

Dad was one of the outraged ones. Before he could say much, Mom – never one to make a public fuss – just said to the Board Chair something like, "We'll find another place and I'll join you for the rest of the meeting."

She and Dad went off to find another lunch place.

Back home over the dinner table, Mom and Dad laughed over the story. They imagined Mom submitting a lunch expense claim from "Joe's Beanery."

Mom did say, "I would have been more upset except that all the men around me were upset."

I understand that never again did the Alberta Opportunity Company book a meeting at that facility. I believe words may have been exchanged.

Years later, I attended an event at that same private club, and women were in the dining room.

~~~~~

It was interesting to me that Mom did a number of things that most women didn't do in that era. She was a pathfinder. But, at least in the early years, she did what she did for the most traditional of reasons – to support her husband.

I suspect also that she could gradually earn credibility because she didn't make a production out of being the first woman. She just quietly went about doing a better job than most people.

I suspect, in some cases, it also helped that Dad was often visibly in the vicinity while Mom played out her non-traditional roles. She was clearly a happily married woman and not, God forbid, an angry feminist. She was clearly not challenging or going against her husband's wishes, and not a threat to anyone's wife.

~~~~~

Mom confided to me once that she was pleased when, in her second year as an AOC board member, on the flight back from a meeting, she happened to sit beside the Board Chair.

He said to her quietly, "Berdie, you do everything right."

She knew what he meant, and treasured that comment.

That was the day Mom said, "I knew I'd been accepted when they stopped being nice to me."

Enjoy music

"You're just in time. I have a job for you," Mom said when I walked into her hospital room. She'd had another heart incident and was going to be in hospital for a while.

My sister Beth and her husband Jim were visiting too. They had been talking about an electric piano for Mom's room at the seniors' lodge.

I was thrilled.

~~~~~

Mom loved music. Growing up in a farming community during the Depression of the 1930s, Mom had happy memories of house parties. Everyone was poor but somehow there was always a fiddle or an accordion and people pushed the furniture out of the way and danced.

When she was 15, Mom moved to town with her sister Edna to go to high school. They boarded with the Capsey family whose daughter Sally taught piano lessons. In those few years, Mom learned to play the piano.

Years later, when I was very little, we lived in an upstairs suite in the house where Mom's parents and her much younger sister Doris lived. I loved listening to Mom and Doris play popular tunes and classical pieces on the piano. Sometimes they'd sing too.

I was beyond excited when I was *finally* old enough to take piano lessons from the same Miss Capsey who'd taught Mom. I practiced on Grandma's piano that Mom and Doris played.

When I was about nine or ten, my parents and grandparents had a falling out and our family moved to a new house on the edge of town. Among all the changes, that meant we no longer had access to a piano. No more piano, no more lessons for me. I was heartbroken.

One day my piano teacher phoned. "I'm sending someone over to see you," she told Mom. A travelling piano salesman was in town. My teacher thought he should visit our home.

When Mom reported this to Dad, he said, "Well, he can come over if he likes, but we're not buying a piano. I'm looking at bills right now and we can't afford a piano."

My heart sank.

The piano salesman turned out to be a slim white-haired older man who appeared to be slightly arthritic. He travelled around in a van with used pianos in the back.

When he arrived, my dad said to him, "Well, you've come at the right time. I'm just going through bills and we can't afford a piano."

To put the next part of the story in context, you need to know that the house we lived in cost $8,000. It was a modest house, but still – you could buy a new house for $8,000.

Dad gestured to a pile of bills and said, "Look at this. I owe $13,000!"

The piano salesman didn't even blink. He said, "You must be an honest man if people will lend you that much money."

He suggested a miniscule monthly payment – possibly for the rest of Dad's life! – and a piano would be ours.

Dad went for it!

I was ecstatic. I thought of it as <u>my</u> piano, though other people played it too. Joyfully, I resumed piano lessons (which, come to think of it, my parents also couldn't possibly afford).

Nobody had to make me practice. The problem was making me stop playing the piano when it was time to do other things.

~~~~~

Looking back with adult eyes, I realize that my parents made big sacrifices so I could take piano lessons. My younger siblings had that opportunity too. Blain didn't enjoy piano lessons much at first but continued into his early teens and also took voice lessons. Beth loved learning to play the piano and continued on into her late teens. Bruce had the opportunity but didn't want to start taking lessons (I think maybe our practicing didn't look fun to him!)

Lessons or not, all four of us absorbed a love of music. Bruce grew up to love blues and roots music and introduced me to Eric Clapton and others of his musical heroes. Blain grew up to enjoy pop concerts, movie themes and pianists like Ferrante and Teicher, Hagood Hardy, Floyd Kramer and Billy Joel (an eclectic mix!). Beth and I love almost any kind of music but especially classical. Beth was even a church organist for many years.

Enjoying music was definitely a gift from Mom. Although Dad loved to dance and liked popular songs from his era, he didn't resonate to music the way Mom did. As Dad's mother once said, "There must be music in him, because none ever came out."

~~~~~

When Mom and Dad built their dream home big enough to accommodate their expanding family, the piano in the family room was well-used. It was not unusual for Mom to be in the family room playing the piano when we arrived for a visit. Any grandchildren or great-grandchildren learning to play were always invited to play something. It was fine if they didn't want to, but important that they know Grandma Berdie would love to hear them play.

Beth and I – who lived a couple of hundred miles apart – enjoyed the opportunity to play piano duets (which, frankly, usually drove everybody else out of the family room).

There are events you attend only because a small relative is participating. (Kindergarten Christmas concerts come to mind.) But as some of her grandchildren and great grandchildren learned to play the piano and join school bands or choirs, Mom actually loved attending their recitals and concerts.

Mom also loved attending almost any kind of concert but especially symphony concerts. As an adult, some of my favourite times with her were attending concerts together.

~~~~~

Mom and Dad loved to dance and it was a treat to watch them have so much fun. They were scrupulous about dancing with other partners too, but it was obvious they were one another's favourite partners.

At their fiftieth wedding anniversary celebration, we were thrilled to be able to invite Mart Kenny – a popular band leader from the thirties and forties when Mom and Dad were courting and then newlyweds. Mart was fifty years older too, but he pulled together a band and we danced the night away to popular jazz tunes from those earlier eras.

Many years after Dad died, Beth and I were visiting Mom. In her living room, some of that old dance music was playing in the background.

Mom told us, "Sometimes when nobody is around, I kind of dance along to that music."

Then she said, shyly, "You know, I don't believe in that three-tier thing – heaven and earth and hell. But sometimes when I'm alone, I imagine that when I die, your Dad will be waiting for me and he will just dance me into heaven."

~~~~~

When Mom moved from her big house to a 14 by 16-foot room in a seniors' lodge, there was certainly no room for her piano. I floated the idea of her getting a compact electronic keyboard, but Mom didn't think it would work.

First of all, she didn't think there'd be room. More importantly, she didn't want to "bother the neighbours" – the others who lived in her wing of the lodge – by playing music they would overhear. Even worse, she thought, she was so rusty that her playing would not be very good. She didn't want anyone to hear.

I pointed out that with an electric piano she could use headphones so nobody but her would hear the sound, but that didn't convince her.

Besides, she said, an electric keyboard wouldn't sound like a real piano.

End of conversation.

~~~~~

So back to the hospital room.

You can understand why I was surprised when Mom announced that she wanted Beth and Jim and me to go to the local music store and find out about electronic keyboards. What changed her mind?

Well, she found out that two people in her wing at the seniors' lodge had electric keyboards in their rooms. One woman didn't even use headphones, but Mom had never ever heard her play. Maybe an electric keyboard wouldn't bother the neighbours.

As well, for Christmas I'd given Mom a CD of music I'd recorded on my electronic keyboard and, she said, "It sounded just like a real piano."

~~~~~

Beth and Jim and I had fun at the music store checking out what kind of electric pianos were available, what features they had, and how much they cost. Mom had specified that she wanted "something that looks like a piece of furniture, not something that looks like an ironing board with a keyboard plunked on top."

Beyond appearance, I was sure I knew exactly what she wanted – just a plain and simple keyboard that you could play like a piano but with headphones so nobody else would hear. No need for bells and whistles to make it sound like a violin or an organ. Certainly no need for percussion that would play different rhythms, or chording that would add background. Nope, I knew she just wanted a keyboard that looked decent.

We found several models with varying features and took the measurements back to her room at the lodge. We found three possible places where a keyboard and a person playing it might fit. Then we reported back to her at the hospital.

~~~~~

I was excited. I knew exactly which one she would pick – an electric piano that was quite beautiful – it looked like a small regular piano – and would simply play piano music.

To my surprise, Mom asked, "Can you make it sound like an organ?"

"I don't think so," I replied. "Is that something you want?"

"Yes," she said. And then I learned for the first time that when Mom was a little girl, her mom – my grandma – had ordered an organ from the Eaton's Catalogue. When it arrived, my grandma and grandpa figured out how to set it up. It was a pump organ, which meant you had to keep pumping pedals to provide air that would allow the instrument to create sound.

My grandma had only about a grade three education because she'd come to Western Canada as a toddler before there were schools. But she had somehow figured out how to play the organ and had taught her daughters too.

"I like the sound of an organ," Mom said.

Her next question surprised me even more. "Does this electric piano have percussion?"

"Do you want percussion?" I asked.

"Well yes," she said. "If you're going to play dance music it's nice to have a little percussion."

So much for me knowing exactly what Mom wanted!

~~~~~

The Saturday the electric piano was delivered and set up by two of Mom's grandsons was a very big day. The keyboard worked! The headphones worked! Mom could play to her heart's delight and nobody else would hear.

A sidebar story made the family rounds: The wife of one of Mom's grandsons knew he was going to "set up a keyboard for Grandma." When the grandson's wife saw the size of the box, she was astonished. "It must be a really big computer," she said. Knowing how much time Grandma spent on the computer, it had not occurred to her grandson's wife that he was setting up a piano keyboard, not a computer keyboard.

From that point on, nearly every time I visited Mom, when I arrived she was playing her electric keyboard. I could tell it was pure joy.

~~~~~

During the last days of Mom's life, it occurred to my sister Beth that Mom might like some music playing softly in the background of her palliative care room.

I was staying in Mom's room at the Lodge, and went in search of some music we could play. I knew any kind of music I found in her room would be something she liked.

Mom had an olden-days portable player that could actually play cassette tapes as well as CDs. When I looked at what was in the player, here is what I found:
- A cassette tape of Beth playing piano and organ music – classical pieces, hymns, and some pop tunes from Mom's era – that Beth had given her many years before,
- A set of CDs of piano music played by four popular pianists, a gift from Blain.
- A CD of piano pieces I had recorded and given to her the previous Christmas.

It was somehow comforting to know that in the last days of her life, she was surrounded by music from her children.

~~~~~

A postscript.

One of Mom's favourite pieces was *Largo* by Handel. As a little girl I loved listening to her play it and was delighted when I was far enough along in my piano lessons to learn to play it too. A few years later, my younger sister Beth also learned to play *Largo*.

Mom often said, "You can play *Largo* at my funeral."

When Beth gave Mom a cassette recording of piano and organ music, Beth included *Largo* as one of the pieces. Years later, when I made a CD recording of piano pieces I thought Mom would like, I too included *Largo*.

At Mom's memorial service, as people were coming in before the service, Beth's and my recordings were the music playing in the background. We both got to play *Largo* at her funeral.

And a few weeks later, at a memorial service at the seniors' lodge where Mom lived her last years, Beth played *Largo* live during the service.

~~~~~

One of the greatest gifts I received from my mom was a lifelong love of music – listening to music, learning to read and play music, singing music in a church choir or around campfires, playing in a school band (trumpet was my instrument).

As a teenager, I poured out my emotions by banging away on the piano when I had no other safe way to express what I felt. I love dancing to music and being immersed in music whether live or recorded. I still have fun figuring out how to create different piano arrangements of tunes I like.

On the inside cover of a CD I created for her, I wrote:

Dear Mom,

Of all the gifts you've given me – starting with being alive! – the gift of music is one that has brought infinite pleasure.

Every day, I am grateful that I got to have piano lessons, and a piano to practice on. As an adult I have a small grasp of the sacrifices you and Dad made to make that opportunity possible.

Music has inspired me, uplifted me, made me cry, made me dance, made me laugh. Every day, I am grateful that I hear music more deeply because of those lessons.

Lately I've begun to play again and I cannot begin to tell you how much delight that brings me.

This CD is a small token of gratitude – played with out-of-practice fingers but immense joy. Thank you, thank you, thank you!

~~~~~

A favourite gift I received at my mother's knee and other joints. My heart sings.

Face it head on

For years, especially after Dad retired and Mom did not, my parents met for coffee every morning at 9:30 at the York Café on Main Street, and every afternoon at 3:15 p.m. at a café called Doughboy's across the street from where Mom worked in the family paper. Sometimes Mom and Dad had coffee with just each other but often friends joined them. They had running jokes and on-going debates. The afternoon coffee group had a game they played to determine who would pick up the tab for coffee. Usually there were lots of laughs.

When our dad died, Mom was home for about a week – the longest she'd ever been away from work except for vacations. On the day she returned to work, she asked my sister and me to meet her at 9:30 a.m. at the York Café on Main Street and at 3:15 p.m. at Doughboy's.

She said, "I want to know that someone will be waiting for me when I arrive. That will make it easier to walk in. I want to face this right now and get it behind me. I don't want there to be places that I'm afraid to go because it's too painful."

~~~~~

Mom once told me, "If there's something I don't want to do, or something that's hard or that I don't like doing, I do that first. Then the rest of the day seems easy."

"Face it and get it behind me" was her operating principle.

~~~~~

For years, my Mom's sisters told her she was crazy to keep living in her big house – the dream house that she and Dad built after the kids left home, to make space for visiting children and grandchildren as the family grew.

Occasionally Mom would say, "I suppose it's kind of silly for one person to live alone in all this space – but I love it!"

She loved the location, backing on to a city park. She loved the home's design, set up to enjoy the view and to provide open spaces for visiting and games, and private spaces for rest and quiet. She loved the furniture and art she'd picked out with Dad, and the practicalities (like a furnace for each floor) that she and Dad had incorporated when the home was being built. She loved having a home and yard big enough for all the family to gather a few times a year.

~~~~~

As Mom's physical condition deteriorated, she gradually arranged for other people to take over more and more care of the house – cleaning and yard care and occasionally major projects like re-shingling the roof.

One of my favourite weekends every year was our annual May trek to greenhouses to pick out flowers for her flower beds and then plant them. Over the years, Mom more and more "supervised" and less and less did any planting, but she could still deadhead and water the flowers on her own.

Eventually, after a hospital stay that left her even more weakened, Mom arranged to have a computer set up so she could work from home, and meals delivered so she didn't have to cook much.

She still cherished her home. Everywhere she looked, something reminded her of happy times; something made her smile.

~~~~~

And then came the most serious "heart incident" she'd ever had. She could barely lift her head from the hospital pillow.

The next morning, frail and weak, she looked up at my brother and me and said, "Well, I guess I have to face the fact that I can't live on my own anymore."

I am so grateful that Mom initiated that conversation. I know families who have agonized when older family members could no longer live safely where they were but refused to move. There is no happy way to deal with the situation.

Sidebar: Our dad actually had to carry his mother, kicking and screaming, out of her home. The combination of her dementia and extremely unsafe conditions in her home meant it would be unconscionable not to move her to a safer place. He took along an old family friend that his mom respected, but it was one of the toughest experiences of Dad's life. Within a few days she was telling others how much she liked the new place, but she never *ever* admitted that to him.

One generation later, lucky us. Our mom was going to "face it and get it behind me."

~~~~~

The next weeks were a flurry of exploring possibilities. Our job was to get information about what was available in the community and report back to her.

Live-in caregiver so she could stay in her home that she loved? Assisted living facility? Eventually she decided that she would actually feel more "intruded upon" in her home with a live-in caregiver than she would in some other facility where she could have some absolutely private space.

Miraculously, a room was available in the facility that she thought she'd like best. She'd have a private room overlooking grass and trees. Meals were provided in a common dining room. Most important from her point of view, she could set up her computer and still work from "home."

~~~~~

So. She moved from her 6,000 square foot dream home (3,000 square feet on two levels) that she had designed and built with our dad, to a 14 by 16 foot room in a seniors' lodge.

A few months after she moved, one of my nieces visited her and reported, "Grandma loves it there."

"Really?" I said. "Did she say that?"

"Yes," my niece said. "When I asked her how she liked it, Grandma said, 'I know it's the best place for me.'"

"Ah," I said and smiled. Mom faced things head on <u>and</u> she was always careful in her wording. "The best place for me" was accurate but didn't mean she didn't miss her home.

~~~~~

When Mom moved into the lodge, she said, "I'm ready to make this move but I'm not ready to put the house up for sale yet."

For a ;while, when out-of-town children or grandchildren came to visit, Mom would join them in staying at her house for a few days.

A highlight event was her annual birthday party. Mom was born on July 1, Canada Day, which is a national holiday. That meant out-of-town family members could usually be available to visit. The family tradition was to gather at Mom's and Dad's home for a July 1 family reunion and birthday celebration. The house was designed for occasions like this, indoors and outdoors.

By the time Mom moved into the lodge, her family of children, grandchildren and their partners, as well as great-grandchildren and great-great-grandchildren, had grown to about 45 people. Even if dinner was catered and we all helped, the logistics of getting the house set up and cleaning up afterwards took a fair bit of organizing, plus actual work.

As well, as Mom grew more frail, she really needed to preserve her energy.

And so one year she announced, "We'll have dinner at Norm's," – a restaurant close to her home that had a private room big enough to accommodate all the family, and a buffet so all of us could eat whatever we chose. The annual killer soccer game took place in a public soccer field before dinner.

Mom wasn't completely happy with the idea that she couldn't be a proper hostess (as she defined it), but she was facing head on what was best in the circumstances.

~~~~~

One day Mom mentioned that she was a little nervous – something I'd not known she ever felt! It was time for her driver's license to be renewed and that required a medical report to confirm she was mentally and physically capable of being a safe driver.

"Going for that medical is like putting my independence on the line," Mom said. She talked about how much it meant to her to be able to drive where she wanted, when she wanted, without having to depend on anyone else. The two parts of that were that she was still independent, and also that she didn't need to "impose on" anyone else.

Her driver's license was renewed.

It was a surprise to me when, a few years later, I learned that, quietly and without fanfare, she decided that she wouldn't be driving any more. Yes, her driver's license was still valid. But she analyzed her health status and decided that it was no longer safe for her to be driving. What if she had a "heart incident" while she was driving? She did not want to be responsible for what could happen.

Face it and deal with it.

~~~~~

And then one day Mom announced, "Okay, I'm ready to put the house up for sale."

The house didn't sell right away (I think that Mom and the rest of the family needed a little more time to say good-bye to it) but eventually the perfect purchaser bought it.

Possession date? Mom suggested 30 days from the day of the sale. The purchaser would have waited but Mom said, "No, let's just get it done." Face it and get it behind her. And so began the intense month of clearing out the home that Mom and Dad had built together.

Once during that month, my daughter-in-law asked Mom, "I've been wondering, is it hard to be leaving this home behind?"

Mom replied, "It's easier because nobody is pushing me. Every step of the way has been my decision." Then she added, as a person who lived in a lodge with many older people, "Some people's children convince them to move when they don't want to."

I thought, *Like any of your children would dare to try to push you!* but I did feel grateful that she was in charge and knew it.

Again, lucky us. We knew that, whatever her diminishing physical capacities, she could and would look after her own best interests. We knew she would face it head on and decide what was best in the circumstances.

~~~~~

One day Mom and I were out for brunch. Mom always picked up the tab, refusing to let others pay, but I said, "Couldn't we at least each pay for our own?"

In response, she said, "You know, the staff at our lodge are wonderful and they do their best, but younger people don't understand that sometimes when you get older you just cannot do the things you used to do."

She continued. "Young people have never been frail. They think they understand but they don't. I've noticed that there comes a time when, as nice as the staff people are, you really need a family advocate."

I was thinking this was an odd response to whether we could share the cost of brunch. I asked, "Are you trying to tell me that the time is getting closer when you might need a family advocate?"

She looked at me like I was really dense and said, "Well it's not getting further away!"

I started to laugh and said, "So are you trying to buy some good will so we'll be family advocates?"

"Well," she said, "Yes."

~~~~~

And that was my mom. Face it head on and do what's best in the circumstances.

Get up, get your lipstick on

"Get up, get your lipstick on, get to work and you won't have time to be sick."

That was Mom's advice for days when we weren't feeling well, and it was her general operating principle for how she ran her life.

As near as I could tell, that operating principle worked for her. In the years when she had four little kids, a just-barely-getting-by weekly newspaper business that started on a card table in my parents' bedroom, worked part time outside our home as well as full time on the fledgling business, helped out neighbours and took part in community activities, Mom's operating principle worked for her.

When I still lived at home, "Get up, get your lipstick on and get to work" was my operating principle too, because on days when I really didn't feel like getting out of bed, I didn't have the courage to say that to my Mom. I didn't think she'd believe I was really sick.

Even if she did believe it, "not feeling well" was not a good enough reason to take a day off. She might say, "Well, you know how you feel," but she would purse her lips and I would feel stabs of guilt for being so irresponsible. "I don't feel like it" was a phrase that had no meaning for my mom.

After I left home and began to take on adult burdens, I too found that "Get up, get your lipstick on and get to work" was a useful operating principle. On more than one occasion when I felt wretched physically or emotionally, I found that when I showered and dressed, got my lipstick on and got out the door, I felt better.

In the years when I was a single mom, always worried about money and struggling to manage full time work, going back to school, and quality time with my children, "Get up, get your lipstick on and get to work" served me well.

~~~~~

Sometime in my forties, I began to learn there were other ways to deal with life's responsibilities and challenges. I was exposed to the phrase, "Work smarter not harder" which caused me to re-think some of the ways I handled my obligations. I wondered if maybe sometimes I worked harder or took on more responsibilities than necessary because I felt guilty if I wasn't pushing full out. I did not discuss that line of thought with my mom.

And then came the time when I was so overwhelmed with life's challenges that I collapsed. The challenges were not workload – in fact, I used work as an escape. The challenges were circumstances in which I lost my identity and questioned everything I ever thought about myself.

It took a long time for me to acknowledge that I couldn't carry on, until one day I started crying and couldn't stop. I discovered, to my horror that – unlike my mother – I couldn't make myself get up, get my lipstick on and get to work. I didn't want anyone to know. Especially not her.

~~~~~

Gradually, by tiny degrees, it filtered into my thoughts that perhaps sometimes, in some circumstances, just maybe, relentless carrying on could be… not helpful. Much later, it occurred to me that sometimes relentless "doing" could even be destructive. I had the completely foreign thought that perhaps sometimes it's good to take a break, withdraw and rest – even if you're not collapsing.

At first the idea of resting or taking a break felt almost like a form of being punished: "Go to your room and don't come out until you can behave."

But later, I began to appreciate that there are seasons and cycles in life. There is a time to work, a time to play, a time for activity and a time for rest – another concept I did not discuss with my mom.

~~~~~

As I moved into my fifties and Mom into her seventies, she did not slow down at all. She continued her full time job at the family paper even after Dad retired from the paper.

When Dad died, we stopped having the conversation about, "Do you think Mom will ever retire?" She now had no reason to retire. Mom continued at the family paper as editor and overseer of the art, accounting, proofreading and reception departments. Her weekly columns were widely read and some years won awards in an international competition.

It seemed to me Mom was ever more skillful at managing tasks and times. She nearly always appeared unruffled no matter how busy the day or week.

At that time, my daughter used to have lunch with her Grandma Berdie on Fridays. The paper was switching to a new accounting system and for six months was running two systems until everyone was certain that the new system worked. That meant double workload for everyone in accounting, including Mom. There were also many other printing and production deadlines.

One Friday, Grandma Berdie was a bit late for her lunch appointment. Uncharacteristically, Grandma was a bit frazzled.

Later, my daughter told me that it was the first time she'd ever seen her Grandma look a bit stressed. My daughter reflected on how she too was stressed at work. Seeing her seventy-plus grandma looking stressed about work, my daughter said, "What hope is there for us?"

~~~~~

As Mom was approaching her eighties, the head of the accounting department was taking a one-year maternity leave. After talking it over with other staff members, Mom made the decision that she and other staff members could cover off the work of that position during the maternity leave year. That seemed a better option than recruiting a new person for the temporary position, spending half a year training the new person and then having to let that person go when the maternity leave ended.

In addition to her continuing full time job, Mom was also now the lead accounting person, not just supervising but doing the work.

From a distance, my observation was that, perhaps for the first time in her life, "Get up, get your lipstick on and get to work" was not working as well for Mom. She actually said out loud in front of other people that she was getting tired. Several times she said she would be very pleased when the accounting staff person returned to work. Then circumstances changed and the accounting person was not able to return to work for many more months than expected.

For the first time in my memory, Mom actually acknowledged that she was perhaps feeling a bit over-extended. She was grateful when the accounting person was able to return, and Mom could go back to her normal role as merely being the editor as well as supervisor of the art, accounting, proofreading and reception departments.

~~~~~

In her mid and late eighties, Mom had a series of "heart incidents." Each one left her a little weaker and a little less mobile. Her mind was sharp and her will was strong, but physically she was declining.

One of the times I brought her home from the hospital and was staying with her until she could be on her own, Mom had a painful realization. When we got to her home, she said, "I'm SO glad to be here."

But she was weak and frail. She just couldn't make the trip from her bedroom, through a corner of the family room, into the kitchen. She could barely shuffle as far as her comfy chair in the family room. Then she had to plop down.

She sat in her chair, completely drained. Her face was grey from the exertion and she took several minutes to recover and catch her breath.

Then she said, in a very weak voice, "You know, when I was young and had four little kids and we were working day and night starting the paper, no matter how tired I was, I could always <u>will</u> myself to do what had to be done. And now I can't."

~~~~~

For the remaining years of her life, I watched in awe as Mom adapted with grace and wisdom to the realities of her declining physical capabilities. The principle of "Get up, get your lipstick on and get to work" changed form but not intent.

She was determined to do all that she could, mentally and physically, but not push herself beyond what was appropriate for her physical condition and her energy level. She knew exactly how much rest she needed, what kind of food made her feel better, and what activities were appropriate for her.

She stopped accepting invitations in advance, saying, "I'd love to go but I won't know until that day if I'm able. Check with me then."

~~~~~

In the last weeks of her life after a series of strokes, she was still doing everything in her power to maintain the abilities she had, and perhaps recover some of the abilities that were now impaired. She who in her younger years could never see the point of exercise would go for walks up and down the hospital hallways in her walker.

As a result of the strokes, her thinking was more scrambled and she had trouble finding words. She told me, "When nobody is around, I sit in my chair and do some exercises, and then I practice thinking." She was pleased that she could remember all the passwords on her computer. She seemed to be rallying and even gaining back some of her capacities.

And then over a weekend she was exhausted.

When my brother and sister-in-law came to visit her Sunday evening, Mom said, "I don't mean to be rude but I have to sleep."

Monday afternoon, something had changed. When she awoke from a nap, she seemed agitated. She wanted, "…something to look at. A p… p… p…."

"A picture?"

"No. P… p… *paper*."

I found a newspaper. She looked at it and was excited. For the first time in weeks, she could actually see the small letters.

She was excited to show me that she could see the letters clearly, large headlines and small text. But as she pointed and said the letters out loud, she was not saying the correct letters.

And then Mom had another realization. The letters had no meaning. She could see the letters but she could not comprehend. She could not read.

That Monday afternoon, the visiting medical specialist recommended a change in her medications, back to one which a few years earlier had caused internal bleeding. (He wouldn't have known that history.) He also ordered more tests. That evening Mom said, "No more poking and prodding."

~~~~~

I'd been staying in Camrose to be with Mom, but that Monday night I had to return to Edmonton for a day and a half. When I left Monday evening, Mom was clearly tired. When I returned Wednesday at noon, I was shocked at how much she had deteriorated.

On Wednesday evening, I asked to speak with the head nurse. I said, "I'm not a medical person and I don't know the physical signs, but it seems to me that our mom is dying. I don't mean she's old and sick and we're all going to die. I mean she seems to be shutting down, actively dying. Am I right?"

The nurse nodded her head.

I phoned my brother and sister to update them. Blain said, "You know, when I saw her Sunday evening, it crossed my mind that this is not the life she wants."

For the first time in my life, I experienced my Mom as not actively exerting herself. A few days later she died peacefully, just one last gentle breath as she slept and slipped away.

~~~~~

A few weeks after Mom died, I still wondered whether – after a lifetime of getting up, getting her lipstick on and getting to work (whatever "work" might mean) – on the Monday she realized that she couldn't read, my mother had given up.

In a meditative state I asked, "Did my mother change her mind about wanting to be alive?"

I will never forget the words that came into my mind.

"No. She didn't change her mind. She opened to a different possibility."

I've been pondering that ever since.

Go down the basement if you're going to crunch your carrots and other timeless sayings

Mom couldn't stand the sound of crunching carrots or celery. I think it made her hair hurt.

She really did say – and it was only partly a joke – "Go down the basement if you're going to crunch your carrots."

It was only partly a joke, but we laughed anyway.

She didn't actually make us go down the basement, but clearly the sound bothered her.

We couldn't figure out how she could possibly eat carrots or celery without crunching, but she did.

Many years later, I had a colleague who described a road trip with mostly men and a few women. One of his friends pronounced, "Women have no bodily functions."

What?

On this trip, men had gastro-intestinal eruptions (farts and burps). Women did not.

Men had to stop for bathroom breaks and snacks. Women did not.

Men got sweaty. Women did not.

My colleague's friend concluded, "Women have no bodily functions."

I laughed and thought it was funny.

But then I thought, "That's true of my mother. She <u>never</u> has a gastrointestinal eruption of any sort – at least not that I've experienced. On long drives, she doesn't need to stop for bathroom breaks or snacks. She doesn't get sweaty. She never has a hair out of place or is in any way untidy. She can eat raw celery or carrots without crunching."

And then I thought, "Good grief! My mother has no bodily functions!"

Wash your face and toidy

Speaking of bodily functions, before we left the house, or before we were going to drive somewhere, the standard instruction was, "Wash your face and toidy."

It got to be a family joke.

One generation later, my sister reported hearing herself say, "Wash your face and toidy" to one of her daughters. Her daughter replied, "But Mo-o-om, I don't *hafta!*"

My sister couldn't remember any of us ever having the wherewithal to think of that.

Jumpy uppy

One of my un-favourite of Mom's expressions was her morning wake-up call. She'd stand at the bottom of the stairs and call, "Jumpy uppy," in a disgustingly cheerful voice.

I hated those words. I hated the cheery tone. I hated having to get up when I was still sleepy.

I still have an aversion to having to get up before I'm fully awake. It takes longer than necessary, because I have to fend off resentment and allow time for my grown-up self to activate.

"Jumpy uppy" indeed. Bah humbug!

Fair is not equal

My mom often said, "Fair is not the same as equal."

She meant that each of us is different. What is a gift to one person (like piano lessons for my sister and me) might be an unpleasant experience for another person (like our youngest brother).

And so, in wanting to be "fair" to others, it's important to understand something about what's important and valuable, or not important or valuable, to each person.

That applies in families. It also applies to how businesses and other organizations can best operate. It applies to public policy.

Fair is not the same as equal. Good to remember.

We just luck out. Be grateful.

Shortly after she moved into a Lodge for older adults who couldn't quite manage on their own any more, Mom reported that often, when someone asked residents, "How are you?" they would reply "Grateful!"

They were just grateful to be alive and breathing for one more day.

Over the years, my observation was that both my parents expressed more and more gratitude for the blessings in their lives. They appreciated the community. They appreciated their family. They appreciated that their lives got easier, compared to their lives during the Depression years and the War years and the early years of struggling to launch a business.

After Dad died, when Mom and I were on a few holidays, delightful unexpected treats would often happen – like finding out we could see a play with Richard Dreyfuss – live! - on that very evening!

Mom would say, "We just luck out!" And she believed we did.

Good way to live.

Laugh

A legendary story when we were growing up was about the time my mom and her sister (my Aunt Edna) were at a lake cottage with their very young children – a three-year-old (that would be me), two toddlers and a baby. (Later, more children would be born to both of them.)

One afternoon it took a long time to settle the children for a nap. When the children were finally asleep, Mom began to read a magazine, and saw a cartoon. In the cartoon, a radio announcer was saying, "We would like to thank our sponsors for their patience during our technical problems, except for Street Brown and Company who were really quite nasty."

That struck Mom funny. She started to laugh. Out loud. Then she got the giggles, and she couldn't stop laughing. Her sister was irked because Mom laughed so loud that she woke some of the babies.

For decades afterwards, our dad could make Mom laugh simply by saying, "What was that cartoon? Street Brown and Company?" She would get the giggles all over again.

And then we'd all start laughing too because our serious do-your-duty mom had uncontrollable giggles.

~~~~~

Mom did like to laugh. She enjoyed puns and satire and clever use of words.

Our dad was a colourful storyteller. She often said about Dad's stories, "He doesn't believe in spoiling a good story with the truth." But she laughed anyway. As we kids grew up and became adults, she appreciated the funny stories we told her about our experiences. She enjoyed laughing at life's foibles.

She enjoyed laughing but she couldn't tell a joke. She liked jokes. She laughed at jokes. But she was bad at telling them.

As a family, we thought the best part any time Mom tried to tell a joke was the way she messed it up.

One joke was, "They spent thousands of dollars to send their son to college and all they got was a quarterback." Mom laughed and thought it was clever. But when Mom told it, she

said, "They spent thousands of dollars to send their son to college and all they got back was twenty-five cents." Then she wondered why nobody laughed.

~~~~~

Just because she couldn't tell a joke didn't mean she had no sense of humour. Once, Dad found a magnet that was a replica of a blue bottle fly. He put it on their fridge. He was really looking forward to Mom's reaction and watching her try to swat it. But she never said anything. She never swatted it. She never even paid attention to it.

After about a week, Dad finally cracked. He had to ask her, "Did you see that fly on the fridge?" Her response? A completely neutral, "Mmmhmm."

She enjoyed driving him nuts by not reacting. Now <u>that</u> was funny!

~~~~~

My brother Blain was especially good at making Mom laugh.

Once when we were kids, when she came home for lunch at noon, she was clearly stressed and irritated about whatever was going on back at the office, plus there was not much time to get everyone fed and out the door back to school and work. She opened the breadbox to find it empty.

"Tell me there isn't any bread," she snapped. I held my breath. She was really angry.

Blain said, "There isn't any bread."

Horrified, I held my breath even more.

Mom looked at him for a moment and then laughed.

The oxygen came back into the room.

~~~~~

Fast forward many decades. Mom was in her eighties and having cataract surgery. My brother Blain was picking her up very early to drive her to where the surgery would take place, about an hour's drive away. It was a bitterly cold blizzardy winter morning with extremely poor visibility and icy driving conditions.

Our mom, who <u>never</u> went out in public without make-up, who even wore make-up when she was home alone, had been told not to wear make-up for the surgery. She was more bothered about going without make-up than she was about the eye surgery.

In his usual helpful way, all during the drive Blain made cracks about how the driving conditions were scary, but it was even more frightening to see his mother without make-up. Of course Mom laughed.

~~~~~

During the night after the surgery, Mom had a "heart incident." She called my daughter (who at that time was the relative living closest to Mom's home) to take her to Emergency. From the hospital, my daughter called Blain.

Mom looked ghastly. Her heart was beating so fast it was actually fluttering, not beating. She was queasy and weak. Her skin was grey.

Blain arrived in Emergency, looked at Mom on the gurney and said, "Well, at least you look better than you did yesterday morning."

The nurse in Emergency looked shocked.

Mom laughed.

Mom couldn't tell a joke, but she did make some funny observations.

For example, our dad was a stickler for safety. At the Booster, he insisted staff wear safety goggles and other gear, and use proper safety procedures for all machinery – especially the power paper cutter. Back home, when he mowed the lawn, he put on coveralls, leather gauntlets and proper work boots. (Underneath the coveralls, he was still wearing his white shirt and tie!) People teased him but he didn't care. Safety was paramount.

When my parents were in their seventies, Dad got up one night to go to the bathroom. On the way back to bed in the dark, he stubbed his toe. He said some words. A voice from the other side of the bed said, "You mean you weren't wearing your steel-toed boots?"

He started to laugh. Then she started to laugh. They both laughed and couldn't stop. When one would begin to wind down, the other would start up laughing again.

Telling the story, Dad said, "There we were, two old coots laughing our heads off in the middle of the night."

It's one of my favourite mental images of my parents.

~~~~~

In her eighties and nineties, Mom had an increasing number of trips to Emergency in the middle of the night. My daughter was most often the person who took her.

Once in Mom's late eighties, someone with a clipboard was asking information to fill out the required hospital forms about her medical history.

One of the questions was, "What was the date of your last menstrual period?"

Mom fired back, "January 23, 1978."

After the hospital person left, my daughter looked at Mom and asked, "Can you really remember the date of your last period?"

Mom just looked over the top of her glasses.

Ah. If someone was going to be so ridiculous as to ask a woman in her eighties about the date of her last period, it deserved a ridiculous answer.

That was Mom's kind of humour.

~~~~~

After Mom was no longer driving, my brother Blain used to drive her to her weekly hair appointment, then pick her up about an hour later.

On one occasion, a problem cropped up at Blain's office, and – totally out of character for my unfailingly reliable brother – it completely slipped his mind to pick up Mom.

About 45 minutes after he was scheduled to pick her up, she phoned him. As soon as he heard her voice, he was horrified that he'd forgotten.

"I was just wondering," she said. "If you're not able to pick me up if you could send somebody with some new magazines because I've pretty much read all the ones here."

~~~~~

Though Mom couldn't tell a joke, she could laugh and did. Her willingness to laugh was a gift to the family. In tough or scary times, it was okay to say something irreverent or something that would get a laugh.

Besides the sheer joy of laughter, I learned it was okay to find humour in dark situations, to use humour to soften a message, to laugh at problems. It's one of my favourite things I learned at my mother's knee and other joints.

Maybe even *because* she couldn't tell a joke!

Love

Mom was not impressed by Hollywood love stories. She was especially contemptuous of interviews or articles by celebrities talking about the great new love of their life.

"Hmp," Mom once said, in response to an actress talking about a new romance. "If they want someone to talk about love, they should ask someone who's been married to the same person for forty years and been through hardships together. That's who knows something about love. Anyone can be excited in the early days when you're still on your best behaviour."

~~~~~

On the eve of my first marriage, Mom gave me two books.

One was a fat olden-days recipe book that told you everything a woman of that era ought to know about cooking for a family: components of a proper meal, how to pluck and clean a chicken, how to set a table for guests when you had no servants, how to make piecrust from scratch…   I read it voraciously and didn't do any of it. Oh yes. It also had recipes.

The second book was about (blush) marital sex. In that era, in that small town, marital sex was officially the only kind that was supposed to exist. We all knew differently, but it wasn't something to be spoken about or acknowledged.

 Mom was clearly uncomfortable, but thought it was her duty to tell me a few things – or at least, to give me the book.

One of the things she said was, "Your father and I seem to have an unusual relationship – based on what I've heard other women say." Though she was not explicit, I got the impression that she actually enjoyed sex, in contrast to other women she knew.

She also once said, with some bemusement, "I never expected to be happy in my marriage. Getting married is just what you did. Being happy wasn't what you expected." Then she paused and said, "It was kind of a nice surprise."

~~~~~

During the time when we were clearing out the home she and Dad built, preparing the house for new owners, we had boxes and boxes of documents and papers – many left by Dad. Sorting them was a big job.

Most documents were simply shredded and recycled. A few that seemed to have some historical value (like Dad's logbooks from World War II) were packed up to be stored in the basement of her grandson who had agreed to store them.

But there was one small box that Mom insisted she needed to have with her in her room at the seniors' lodge. It was a box of letters – written on lightweight parchment paper – that she and Dad had exchanged while he was overseas during the war.

She knew that eventually, after she died, that box of letters would join the other documents in her grandson's basement, but she wanted him to understand something. She tied the box of letters with thin ribbon – in knots.

She said, "I don't want to throw these away. But I don't want anybody to read them."

After a pause, she said, "They're too raunchy."

Then she added, "Especially for grandchildren."

~~~~~

A few weeks after Dad died, I was speaking with one of Mom's oldest and dearest friends. The friend commented on how much Mom must be missing Dad. Then she said about my parents, "They were still lovers. Most of us move on and have something that is quite nice, but we're not lovers any more. Your mom and dad were still lovers."

The rest of us could tell. As kids, we could feel the spark of electricity between our parents, though we didn't have words for it when we were little. We always knew that, though our parents loved us, they were Number One in each other's eyes. After nearly 51 years of marriage, they were still flirting.

Once at a family gathering in their home, when my parents were in their seventies, my teenage daughter came around a corner and stumbled on Grandma and Grandpa locked in an embrace and kissing. My daughter was mortified. A couple of decades later, telling of that experience, she said, "Now I'm old enough to think, 'Good on ya,' and hope I should be so lucky when I am that age."

~~~~~

I once said to Mom, "Must be nice to live with someone who tells you every day that you're beautiful and that he loves you."

"Ye-e-es, I suppose," she said. "But sometimes I think, talk is cheap."

I'm sure I raised my eyebrows.

~~~~~

Quick diversion.

Historically, we all knew that, when Mom and Dad first married, Dad announced that he would not be helping with housework. He would explain to us (with a halo over his head), that he didn't mean that she had to do it. He was fine if she wanted to get help with housework, or not do it, or whatever. It's just that he wasn't going to do it.

The fact that until the later decades of their marriage they had no money to get help was irrelevant.

Dad also considered himself a champion of women's equal place in society. In many ways he was. But that didn't extend to changing traditional roles around the house.

No disconnect in his mind!

~~~~~

Back to Mom saying, "…talk is cheap."

She went on to say that, on mornings when she was at work and Dad was at home, she'd come home for lunch. Dad was there, possibly lying on the couch. She would make lunch for them both, tidy up afterwards and then go back to work.

She said, "I know if our positions were reversed, I would make his lunch."

And still, clearly their marriage was good for both of them. They loved each other, liked each other, had fun together, and after fifty-plus years, still had a spark between them.

~~~~~

Mom loved Dad deeply and passionately, but she was not sentimental.

That applied to others she loved too. When we were growing up, our community had the custom of Decoration Day. On a Sunday in August, people would go to the cemetery and place flowers on the graves of people they had lost.

Mom commented that she went every year and placed flowers on her father's grave, but she only did that because it mattered to her mother. After her mother died, our mom didn't do the Decoration Day ritual anymore.

"I don't care about memorials," Mom said. "I care about what's in my heart and my memories."

In the days after our dad died, we saw that perspective in action. She wasn't concerned about long-term memorials but she was considerate about the sensibilities of Dad's children and grandchildren.

She checked with each of us four children to see if any of us had objections to Dad being cremated. We did not

She also thought about how Dad's grandchildren might want to remember him. She decided that during the few days before the memorial service, anyone who wished would be able to view his body at the funeral home.

"I know it seems extravagant since he's going to be cremated," she said, "But I'd like him to wear his tuxedo. He had so much fun wearing it." As well, a few years before he died, shortly after he purchased his tuxedo, Dad had given each of his grandsons a tuxedo for Christmas.

I will not forget being in the room during one of Mom's meetings with the funeral director. He wended his way around to, "What would you like to do with the ashes?"

Mom looked him in the eye and said, "Whatever you like."

It took the funeral director a minute to understand. She had no interest in what happened to Dad's ashes. That wasn't him. She had what was in her heart, and the memories.

~~~~~

The year after Dad died, I had the heart-sinking job of telling Mom I was leaving my husband.

I was dreading the conversation.

Here was a woman who as far as I could tell had a good marriage for more than fifty years with a man that many considered to be difficult.

And here was I, about to tell her that I was going to leave my husband. My second husband.

I was sure Mom would disapprove.

She listened quietly. And what she said next surprised me.

She said, "I don't think he kept any of his promises."

She went on to tell me a couple more of her observations about the husband I was leaving. "Even during your wedding ceremony," she said, "he was joking around. Your Dad and I thought he didn't take the vows seriously."

In all the years I'd been together with this man, I had no idea she had reservations. She was gracious always.

That didn't mean she was being phony. She believed in being gracious. The other thing was, she concluded that telling me her real opinions would only drive a wedge between us, and she wanted to be sure that she and Dad could be on hand to help if necessary.

~~~~~

And then she told me this story.

Once, when I would have been in my early teens, our dad was being particularly difficult. He was angry and argumentative all the time. I remembered that time, and how we all tried to stay out of his line of vision. As an adult, I was also aware of some of the enormous stresses they faced in their business which was still struggling to survive. Mom and Dad were both working day and night, and of course Mom was also looking after the household and the children.

Mom said, "One day I thought I just couldn't take it anymore. I went out to the golf course and stomped around the entire course. And at the end of it, I just couldn't figure out how I could swing it on my own with four little kids. I decided I would just have to figure out how to make things work."

I was astonished.

And then I was grateful. Mom was not telling me this story as a message to "suck it up." She was telling me that she would have left her husband if it had in any way been feasible.

I began to stop idealizing my parents' marriage.

One other thing. Up to that point, at age 50, as far back as I can remember I always thought my mother disapproved of me and that I was a disappointment to her. The day she told me about stomping around the golf course might have been the first day in my life that I <u>felt</u> my mother's love for me.

As my sister Beth has said, "Nobody grows up in the same household."

I grew up believing love was always conditional on me measuring up – and I never did. My sister Beth grew up believing she was loved no matter what. How could that be?

Beth told me a story. My memory of the story she told is that at about age six or seven, Beth had done something wretched and Mom was chastising her. Beth said, "I hate you!"

Mom's response: "You can be angry with me if you like but I will always love you."

Hearing that story, I agreed with Beth than nobody grows up in the same household!

(All these years later, Beth remembers the story differently. She says she would never have dared to say "I hate you" to our mother.)

~~~~~

Yes, Mom's way of expressing love was steady and reliable. Also passionate, when it came to Dad. And yet…

She could make you want to shrivel up and die.

My siblings and I have talked about it. Dad was often terrifying. Mom was in some ways worse. "I'm very disappointed in you" could make me feel like dying of guilt.

That didn't go away just because we became adults.

Once when I brought her home from hospital and was staying with her for a few days, it seemed I couldn't do anything right. Everything I did was wrong, and not just the things I did to try to help her. Everything about <u>me</u> was wrong. Example: "You eat too much."

There I was, an adult old enough to be called a "senior." And there I was – again – beginning to feel like a completely defective human being.

When another family member finally arrived to stay with her, I could hardly wait to get out of there. I barely said "Good-bye" and just fled.

~~~~~

As far as I know, Mom mostly confined her ability to make people guilty or obligated to those of us within the family. But not always.

At one point, she was helping to raise money so that our local college could build a university-caliber library. One of the people on her contact list was a man she'd known since he was born. He was the son of a woman who taught Mom at the one-room schoolhouse she attended as a child.

At the time of the college library fundraising campaign, the man had been a pharmacist and drug store owner for decades, an elected Camrose City Alderman, and was well respected in the community.

When Mom phoned and asked if she could visit to talk about the library, he and his wife talked it over. They decided Mom could visit, but they were not going to contribute.

When Mom arrived, she looked around at their gracious home and said, "My, your mother would be proud."

She reminded him that his mother had been her teacher in the one-room schoolhouse (like he would forget).

"I can see that you have lots of books," she said. "And you know, we didn't have books in that one-room schoolhouse. Books are so important for learning."

Telling the story, the man laughed and said, "I just went in the next room and got my cheque book."

~~~~~

Once in my sixties, in a mastermind group of fellow entrepreneurs, I was moved to say, "I could never do that. If I did, my mother would purse her lips and then I would die."

Everybody laughed and I did too.

But it wasn't really a joke. My mother was still alive, and it still mattered to me what she thought.

Several years later, a few months after Mom died, my sister discovered a short video of an interview with Mom. In the video, Mom was in her living room in front of the brick fireplace, commenting on something she thought was important. Watching the video was a surreal experience. It really did capture Mom's essence.

I forwarded the video clip to a woman who'd been in the mastermind group with me and who'd become a close friend. She watched it and said, "I can see why you were afraid of your mother pursing her lips!"

~~~~~

Yes, with her implacable rightness and her streak of judgementalness (even though she genuinely believed in tolerance), she could make me want to shrivel up and die.

And yet and yet…

Once after one of Mom's heart incidents, she was in serious enough condition that the hospital staff placed her in a room with a large window they could see from the nursing station.

I don't think it was intended to be a hospital room. It was more like a storage area. A hospital bed had been rolled into the room but there was no bedside table and no place to hang clothes. Hospital equipment was shoved into various places. Worse, with the large window visible to the nursing station, the room had no privacy.

When I walked in to visit her, I thought, "What an ugly uncomfortable room!" Knowing how much it mattered to Mom to be surrounded by tidiness and beauty, and how fiercely she protected her privacy, I thought the surroundings would bother her.

She was lying on her back with her eyes closed, and I thought she might be asleep. But when I said, "Hi Mom, this is Bonnie," she smiled, still with her eyes closed.

After a moment, she said in a weak voice, "I've been lying here thinking."

I wondered if she might comment on her surroundings.

And then she said, "I've been thinking how much love there is in the world."

Oh.

"…And how much kindness," she continued. "So many people have been so kind to me in the last few days."

After a few seconds, she slowly turned her head to face me, and opened her eyes.

"And I know you worry about not visiting me as often as you think you should," she said.

I felt tears spring to my eyes.

Then she said, "You don't need to worry about that. I know you visit as often as you can. And I know you love me. You don't have to tell me. And I hope you know that I love you."

She paused for a moment and then said, "I hope everybody knows I love them."

~~~~~

I hope so too.

Put your face on

Mom might be the only person I've ever known who wore make-up even when she was home alone. She wouldn't dream of going out in public without make-up and what she considered to be proper attire for being in public. Even when she was home alone, she dressed properly. After all, you never knew when someone might drop by.

As a child and teenager living at home, I seldom saw Mom without make-up, and then only very early in the morning. She'd say, "Got to put my face on."

~~~~~

In my ratty adolescent stage, and later in my "I'd be a flower child if only I didn't have kids" stage, I considered her "keep up appearances" mentality to be a form of vanity. Seemed to me it was putting on a phony front.

She did not see it that way at all.

She wanted to be at her best when she was with others. "Putting her face on" was one way of showing people they were important to her.

She quoted the Queen Mother. During World War II in London England, King George VI and his wife Queen Elizabeth would go out into the streets of London to visit people that had been bombed. The Queen always dressed elegantly.

Once a man said to her, "You're very dressed up." The Queen replied, "Of course. Wouldn't you get dressed up if you came to visit me?"

He laughed and said, "I guess I would."

That was Mom's attitude. Putting her face on and being properly dressed was a form of showing respect.

~~~~~

Mom had a sense of style that made her look good even when the family had no money for discretionary expenses like clothes. She didn't necessarily have the latest fashion, but she had an eye for choosing classic line, colour and fabric that suited her and didn't go out of style.

She mentioned one day that she was glad her "good dress" – the one she wore to church and any special occasion – was a colour and fabric that was appropriate twelve months of the year. She felt sorry for one of the neighbour ladies whose "good dress" was clearly a summer colour, but had to be worn in the winter too.

~~~~~

Dad enjoyed the fact that Mom always looked good.

In the years after the kids left home, the *Booster* found its feet and money got easier. Dad often bought Mom a classy dress for her birthday or Christmas. Mom had a favourite dress shop, and the owner was brilliant at helping Dad pick out something that fit Mom perfectly and looked good on her.

One dress I particularly remember. It was definitely a New Year's Eve dress in the years when people got glitzy-dressed-up for New Year's Eve parties. The dress was practically backless. I don't think Mom would ever have chosen it herself, but it was a gift from Dad, and that's what she wore on New Year's Eve.

She looked spectacular.

~~~~~

Another spectacular dress was the one she wore at their 50th wedding anniversary party. The top was black velvet with a straight neckline and long sleeves. The torso of the dress was cut low and diagonally over her hips. The bottom was white and frothy, also cut diagonally, parallel to the top. She wore a gorgeous white orchid corsage. The whole ensemble was the epitome of understated elegance.

One of my favourite photos is of Mom in that dress and Dad wearing his tuxedo, dancing up a storm at their 50th Wedding Anniversary party.

Many years later, my sister Beth was able to wear that elegant dress at her 50th Wedding Anniversary party.

Fond memories.

~~~~~

In the last few months of Mom's life, I knew she was failing when she stopped wearing make-up.

She said there were two reasons. First, she couldn't stand very long in front of a mirror.

The second reason was that, because she couldn't see properly without her glasses, she was afraid she would "look like a clown with make-up smeared all over my face."

Hmmm. Being seen in public without her face on. A radical change.

One day I noticed another radical change. Mom had shoved her feet – without socks – into a pair of slip-on shoes.

This was a woman who did not have bare feet even when she wore sandals. In sandals, she'd wear little footlets so her bare feet were not actually touching the leather in the sandals.

Noticing me noticing her bare ankles, she explained it was just too difficult to put on socks.

No make-up and no socks? I knew for sure she was failing.

~~~~~

Failing but not fallen.

For decades, Mom had a standing weekly hairdresser appointment. Her hair was always tidy; never a hair out of place. She wore the same style she'd worn in the 1950s but somehow on her it didn't look out of fashion. It was just her.

On the day she came out of surgery, her biggest concern was the "moptop" that her hair had become. During her last hospital stay, she was SO uncomfortable that she hadn't had her hair done for several weeks.

I checked with the hairdresser shop she'd been going to every week for decades. Yes, they were willing to come to the hospital and do her hair if the hospital would give permission.

I checked with the head nurse who said, "Heavens yes! Nothing makes you feel better than having your hair done." (A woman after Mom's heart!).

And so, with the help of her faithful hairdresser and a little juggling of furniture and extension cords for plugging in a hair dryer, Mom had a shampoo and set.

She felt SO much better.

Set the bar high

When I was about 10 years old, Mom agreed to be Superintendent of the Sunday School at our church.

About a year before that, Mr. Schnell had retired as Superintendent of the Sunday School, a volunteer position he had held for many years. He was a wonderful man, generous, kind and friendly. For all those years, the Sunday School percolated along smoothly without much change.

At an appointed time in the weekly church service, the minister would ask the children and teenagers to leave the adults' service and go to Sunday School in the church basement. There, we children would have a little time together for some songs and short comments led by Mr. Schnell, and then we'd move to classes with others our age, led by volunteer teachers.

Most people in the congregation didn't think much about the Sunday School. It was just something running smoothly in the background – a way to get restless children out of the adults' church service.

~~~~~

When Mr. Schnell retired, the church leaders scrambled to find a replacement superintendent. Nobody volunteered. A few people who had been Sunday School teachers agreed to "help out for a while" until a replacement was found. Those teachers asked a few other people to help out with some of the classes. Requests were along the lines of, "We just need someone to cover off until we find a new superintendent and teachers. It's only about an hour a week of your time. Would you help fill in?"

Things went downhill. Fewer and fewer volunteers participated. Things came to a head one Sunday morning when no adults at all showed up at Sunday School. Bands of children were roaming around the church basement unsupervised and noisy. At that point, the church leaders announced that Sunday School would be suspended until the next fall.

~~~~~

Enter my mother. In response to pleas from the minister, she agreed to take on the role of Sunday School Superintendent. For me as a kid, Mom's new responsibility was just something going on in the background. As an adult, I know that before she said "Yes," Mom would have given thought to whether she could or should take on this challenge and how she would approach it.

Once taken on, she was fully committed to doing the best job possible.

~~~~~

I wasn't paying attention, but I do remember hearing her phone conversations as she began to recruit people to help with Sunday School.

I was aware she had hand-picked people she thought would do a good job. Her phone conversations went something like this.

"I'm phoning to ask if you would take on a very important job. The job is to be a Sunday School teacher. This is a really important job. It's teaching our children about what we believe in. I wouldn't ask just anyone, but I'm asking you if you would consider it. I don't want you to decide right now. I'd like you to think about it for a few days before you decide."

If the person didn't say "no" right then, Mom would continue.

"It's not just an important job, it's a big job. If you agree to do it, here's what you'll need to do. You'll need to spend a few hours each week preparing for your Sunday lesson."

She'd continue, "On Sunday mornings, you'll need to arrive early for church and check to make sure your classroom is ready for the children. You'll be teaching your class during Sunday School time. After church, you'll need to stay for a while in case one of the children or parents wants to speak with you, and you'll need to watch that each of the children leaves with a responsible adult."

After a pause for a few comments from the person on the phone, Mom would lay out more expectations.

"Also, there's a new curriculum this year. All the teachers will be meeting with me once a month to make sure we're on track with the new curriculum."

Then she'd add even more.

"If for some reason you need to be away on a Sunday, it will be your job to arrange for a substitute teacher and make sure that person knows what's expected. You'll also let me know who the substitute teacher will be."

~~~~~

Mom's closing comments were something like, "I think you would be excellent at this important job and I'd be honoured to have you on our team, but I don't want you to decide right now. I'd like you to think about it for a few days before you decide if you are able to make this commitment."

I now appreciate more than I did then of how she respected and valued the worth of people she spoke with while laying out clear expectations. It worked with us kids and it worked for adults too.

Mom would end with what I now understand as the "confirm commitment" stage of a sales call. "I'll phone you back on Tuesday to see what you've decided."

~~~~~

Over the dinner table, I listened to Mom report to Dad how she was coming with her recruitment effort. Of the people she asked, nearly all agreed to take on the job. In August she began holding meetings to help the teachers prepare for Sunday School opening in September.

During the years she was Superintendent, Sunday School attendance went up, no class was ever without a teacher, and the entire congregation began to appreciate that Sunday School was more than just a way to get restless children out of the adults' church service.

Mom didn't ever explain her logic, but I do remember her saying something like, "If you ask people to do something big and important and tell them exactly what you expect, they'll usually rise to the occasion. And if they say 'no' you're better off without them."

Good lesson that served me well when I became an adult.

Shut the cupboard doors

In 1952, *The Camrose Booster* weekly paper was launched on a card table in my parents' bedroom. Later it expanded into the basement, and for several years staff came to our home. I remember falling asleep to the sound of a printing press in the basement.

It was a 625 square foot storey-and-a-half home, with two adults and four children living on the main floor and half-upstairs, and some days a crew of eight people working in the basement. A tad crowded, not to mention not much privacy for the family.

The kicker was the Christmas morning when someone came to our home to place a classified ad.

Time to move to commercial space.

~~~~~

When the business moved from the basement of our home to commercial space downtown, Mom was no longer home when we four kids got home from school. Every day after school she would phone to check in on us.

Mom would make sure she heard all our voices or knew exactly where we were. She would give instructions to wash the lunch dishes in the sink (there was never time to do that at lunchtime). She'd tell us how to start supper and perhaps do other errands.

And then she would say, "…and shut the cupboard doors and put the lid on the peanut butter."

We'd glance around and think, "How does she know?"

That was a motivator to make sure we did whatever she had asked, and to behave as if she could see what we were doing. Maybe she could!

~~~~~

So what did I learn from that?

Right off the top, I came to believe that my mother was omni-present and omni-powerful (not that I knew those words at the time). I decided I'd better always act in a way she'd approve. I figured that if I didn't, *she would know* and the consequences of that were too scary to contemplate.

I didn't actually imagine any particular punishment. Just the thought of Mom's disapproval was terrifying.

From there, I kind of assumed that all adults in positions of authority probably knew exactly what I was doing even if they couldn't physically see me.

Reflecting all these decades later, that was one of many factors (most notably my own natural inclinations) that led to a few decades where my main goal in life was always to please others, or at least to avoid their disapproval.

~~~~~

The other thing I learned? Tidy is more pleasant than messy. She sometimes said, "The difference between a tidy house and a messy house is about ten minutes."

She was right. With just a few motions, it's possible to make an environment more pleasant. My physical spaces are not always tidy, but I've learned that a simple thing like shutting the cupboard doors can greatly improve how a room looks and feels. That in turn improves my state of mind.

~~~~~

One other incident.

Sometime in my twenties, I lived with my two little kids in an upstairs suite that overlooked a lot full of used farm machinery. One day I was looking out the window and saw a boy wander onto the lot and start to climb one of the pieces of equipment.

I shouted down, "Stop that! Get down!"

The boy looked around and couldn't see where the voice came from.

I shouted again, "Get down!"

He looked unnerved, and actually climbed down and left the lot, still glancing behind to see where the voice was coming from.

I figured he might have thought it was The Voice of God.

I had a moment's fleeting glee and wondered if that's how Mom felt when she said, "…and shut the cupboard doors."

Watch your numbers

Mom loved numbers. She was good at numbers. She did math in her head. Numbers spoke to her.

She counted all kinds of things. She didn't *decide* to count things. Her mind just did that.

Walking someplace with a stairway? She'd report the number of steps when we reached the top. She just couldn't help counting them.

After we'd been to an event, she'd say, "There were 126 people. Ten rows of thirteen seats each, and four empty chairs."

Sometimes she'd laugh and say something like, "I don't remember much of what the speaker said, but I can tell you how many people were in the audience."

~~~~~

From the beginning of when she and Dad launched *The Camrose Booster,* they were rigorous about keeping up-to-date financial records. Mom was the bookkeeper.

This was in the olden days – no accounting software, no spreadsheets, no hand-held electronic calculators. The bookkeeping tools were a paper ledger, a pen or pencil to write entries, and a mechanical adding machine, slightly smaller than a typewriter.

Each week Mom made manual entries in the ledger of expenses and income. Each week she balanced the books.

When I got to be a teenager, she taught me to help with the bookkeeping. I learned about debits and credits and double-entry bookkeeping. If there are no errors, the total credits will equal the total debits, and the books are said to be "balanced."

I learned about income and expenses, receivables and payables, interest on debts, and a whole lot of other things that came in useful in later years when I became a manager and then started a business.

I also learned the frustration when the books didn't balance. Mom had a system for how to check entries and adding machine tapes looking for errors. She also had tricks to check where an error might be.

If the difference between the debit total and credit total was divisible by nine, that meant somewhere in the entries was a figure reversal. If the difference between debit and credit totals was an even number, the error could be that something that should have been posted as a credit was posted as a debit or vice versa.

Sometimes the error or errors did not reveal themselves quickly. You would not have wanted to be around Mom during one terrible week when for several days she couldn't balance the books. I don't remember how many days that went on, but I do remember trying to stay out of her way.

~~~~~

Being up to date with weekly books was important but Mom also noticed other things about the numbers. Dad told stories about how Mom would look at the ledger of that week's balance sheet and point out something she thought was fascinating.

"Would you look at that?" she'd say. "Every one of the totals is divisible by nine," or "The credit totals all have a six in them but none of the debit totals do."

Dad cared a great deal about the story the books were telling. ("Did we make any money? How's our cash flow?") I gathered from his laughter that he did not share her fascination with the numbers themselves.

~~~~~

Mom's connection with numbers extended beyond counting and bookkeeping. As a proofreader, she read all the classified and display ads in each week's paper. Many advertisers had ads every week. Over time, she remembered the phone numbers and addresses of all the regular customers.

She laughed at herself. If I mentioned the name of a regular classified ad customer – say, someone who advertised rental suites every week – she'd say, "It's kind of embarrassing. When they come in every month to pay their bill, I remember their phone numbers but I don't remember their faces."

~~~~~

As technology changed, there came a time when the *Booster*'s manual bookkeeping system went electronic. Mom was in charge of working with the company that designed their custom accounting program. She may not have been a software expert, but she knew what the system had to be able to do. She was rigorous working with the vendor until everything worked perfectly.

Technology changed again, and a new accounting system was implemented. Under Mom's supervision, working directly with the vendor, for six months – with considerable labour – the *Booster* ran both the old and new accounting systems. That lasted until she was confident no further glitches remained and the new system could do all the functions it needed to do.

The accounting systems also had multiple back-ups. Every night for years, Mom personally carried home the briefcase containing tapes that held up-to-the-minute financial records. Every morning she took the briefcase back to the office. Not for her relying solely on digital back-ups in off-site locations. The *Booster* records needed a physical back-up too.

~~~~~

Mom's record-keeping continued to the end of her days. After she died, clearing out her room at the Lodge, I found her personal ledgers.

Banks, investment companies and vendors sent statements, but Mom kept her own paper record of everything. In her cursive handwriting, she wrote all the numbers – in pen! –and did her own calculations. Heaven help any bank or vendor that made an error. Mom would find it. She would of course be courteous and gracious, but the error would be corrected to her satisfaction.

She knew to the penny her income and expenses, and the status of her investments.

And I'm guessing she never stopped noticing and saying to herself, "Well, would you look at that?" when she saw something in the numbers that she thought was interesting.

Watch your words

In addition to being a number person, Mom was a word person. She lived by and for words.

She was meticulous about vocabulary, spelling, grammar and punctuation. As hawk-eyed proofreader and editor at the *Camrose Booster,* she could spot a grammatical error at a hundred paces. She cringed at typos. I think spelling errors caused her actual physical pain.

One of Mom's favourite books was *Eats, Shoots and Leaves*[1] – a book about punctuation. For months after she first read it, every time someone visited, she'd read a quote from the book.

Whenever the *Camrose Booster* was hiring someone as a typist writer, or a graphic artist who created ads, Mom's infamous spelling test was one of the hoops applicants had to jump through. (Oops, that should have been 'hoops through which applicants had to jump.') The test consisted of words that are frequently misspelled.

In Mom's view, if you were going to work for a paper you ought to know that "accommodate" has two "m's." You ought to know the difference between "cite," "sight" and "site."

(If you don't know the difference, that's okay. You undoubtedly have other sterling gifts. Just don't try to get a job at the *Camrose Booster*.)

My brother Blain, properly appalled, tells the story of an applicant with a University degree in English who applied for a writing job at the *Booster*. Like all applicants, she took the infamous spelling test. Her score was 27 out of 50. An English major! Much clucking of the tongue.

---

[1] Lynn Truss (2003): *Eats, Shoots and Leaves: The Zero Tolerance Approach to Punctuation.* Gotham Books, Penguin Group (USA) Inc.

What further appalled Blain was the former elementary school teacher who said, "Spelling doesn't really matter." Blain thought that helped explain why so many Grade XII graduates could not spell or write a proper sentence.

Mom applied her same high standards to anyone who did any kind of writing. Once, during what I thought was going to be a friendly family phone chat, she pointed out my incorrect use of "principle" versus "principal."

~~~~~

Mom could use words to make pungent observations.

Once Dad had, in her opinion, taken up much too long speaking at a meeting.

Later when I was having coffee with them, he said, "You say a few words you think are helpful and she's mad."

She gave him her cool look and said. "I don't think I've ever objected to a few words."

I thought it was funny. Dad was less amused.

Another time, one of Mom's young adult granddaughters was getting a ride home with Grandma. The granddaughter had encountered several people who annoyed her that day, and spent most of the ride complaining about them.

Mom drove and listened without comment until her granddaughter stopped ranting. Then she – who almost never used "bad language" in public – said, in a very level voice, "It's been my observation that if I encounter three bastards in one day, the problem is not with them."

Twenty years later, the granddaughter still tells that story, and how it turned her mind around somewhat.

~~~~~

Mom also wrote "Pen Points," an award-winning weekly column. Years after she died, I still meet people who tell me they miss her thoughtful clear-thinking columns.

On one occasion, she wrote about a situation that was causing local controversy. She told me that people on both sides of the issue called her to say, "Berdie, you got it right."

That pleased her – not just the writing, but that it might make a difference in the community.

Once, in her last few years, after she'd moved to an assisted living facility but was still proofreading and writing her weekly column, she phoned me.

"I just have to tell someone," she said.

She'd learned that, in the "best original writing" category in the Independent Free Papers of America (IFPA) annual competitions, her Pen Points column had received an award. There would have been hundreds or even thousands of entries from papers across the US and Canada, so this was indeed an honour.

Mom had won the award a few times before, but this was special. "I know I'm not as sharp as I used to be," she said, "so I didn't think I'd win it again."

I was thrilled for her. "Did you tell the ladies at your dining table?" I asked.

"No," she said. "They wouldn't understand." I knew she also wouldn't have wanted to seem like she was bragging.

She laughed and added, "That's why I had to phone you."

~~~~~

Mom enjoyed puns and word games and crossword puzzles, but her absolute favourite word game was Scrabble. If she was playing, we called it Killer Scrabble. She was a formidable player – both defensively and offensively – but always gracious.

I found it particularly irritating when, just before she plunked down a 7-letter word with a Q and a Z on a triple and was about to get a gazillion points, she'd say, "I'm sorry to have to do this…"

Yeah right.

In later years, Mom's ability with words got to be an indicator. If I beat Mom at Scrabble more than twice in a row, I did not feel jubilant. I was worried. That meant something was off.

She once confided to me that she knew something was wrong with her health. Three days in a row she was not able to get all the words in the daily newspaper's crossword puzzle. We both knew that meant something was seriously wrong.

It turned out she was bleeding internally – a side effect of one of her medications.

~~~~~

In the last weeks of Mom's life, after what appeared to be several mini-strokes and also after a surgical procedure, she had trouble accessing words. That bothered her.

A speech therapist came to visit and explained that, after a stroke, people often have trouble finding words. "They might be trying to say 'pen' and they know what they're trying to say but the word just won't come out," the speech therapist explained.

"Yes," I said. "Mom had that difficulty earlier today. Except, she was trying to say, 'macular degeneration.'"

"Oh," the speech therapist said. She laughed, set down her clipboard and began to speak to Mom and me in an actual conversation.

~~~~~

In the last weeks of Mom's life, one of the toughest incidents was the day Mom was excited to realize that she could see letters again. No more double vision or fuzziness.

But as she began to point to letters and name them, I could see that she was not naming them correctly.

I was beside her as she came to the realization that, although she could see letters, the letters had no meaning to her. Her stroke-impaired brain could not comprehend. My mom, the woman who lived by and for words, could not read.

~~~~~

But.

She'd already established her word legacy.

It was not just her ability to spot a grammatical error at a hundred paces, or her precise vocabulary, spelling and punctuation. It was not just her hundreds of Pen Points columns or her Killer Scrabble game or her generous support of literacy and libraries.

She left behind a few generations of word people. Among her children, grandchildren and great grandchildren are people who enjoy words. Many of us delight in word games and puzzles and puns. We can express ourselves with words, spoken and sometimes written.

Some families have generations of athletes. Some are fabulous at mechanics or law or construction or medicine. Some have generations of teachers or farmers or musicians. Our family seems to have generations of people who are good with words. We just can't help it.

Somewhere in the cosmos, right this second, I can feel the spirit of my mom, proofreading this chapter.

When one door closes…

"I have always believed," Mom said, "that when one door closes, another one opens."

It was one of the days immediately after Dad died.

"But this time…," she said. She paused for what seemed like a long time and then she almost whispered.

"This time… I don't see how that can be."

Neither did I. I could almost hear doors clanging shut. Dad's death felt like thousands of endings.

But until that day, Mom had stories to demonstrate that when one door closes, another one opens.

~~~~~

Once when I was very scared and discouraged, Mom told me this story.

Early in the Second World War years, Mom and Dad were married, aged 19 and 22. Less than a year later, like most other young men of the era, based on what was happening in Europe, Dad concluded that it was his duty to enlist. He joined the Royal Canadian Air Force.

For the first few months after Dad enlisted, Mom was able to travel with him to the places in Alberta where he was posted. Then came the day when he was posted to an unnamed location, probably on the way to being sent overseas.

Mom said the day Dad left was one of the worst days of her life. She didn't know where he would be, or when or if they would ever see each other again. She was pregnant. She wondered if he would ever see their little child. A door had closed.

~~~~~

A few days later she saw one of the other young wives, who said she'd heard the men might be at a military base in

Calgary – still in Alberta. The two young women decided to get on a bus and see if they could find their husbands somewhere on the base.

They did find their two husbands. When Dad saw Mom, he said, "Sweetheart!" Hugs and kisses ensued. The other husband said, "What the hell are you doing here?" and that couple went off fighting.

Mom felt doubly blessed that she got to see Dad and that they were so happy to see each other.

It turned out that for the next two years, Dad's postings were all in Canada and Mom was able to travel with him. Not only did Dad get to see his first child (that would be me) but he got to see my brother Blain who was born during that time too.

Even when things look black, there's hope. When one door closes, another one opens.

~~~~~

And then there was our family's Black Friday (named after the 1920s Stock Market Crash Black Friday, not the shopping day after American Thanksgiving Black Friday).

Our Black Friday was the ultimate demonstration that when one door closes, another one opens.

About six or seven years after the war ended, my dad got the germ of an idea to start a weekly paper that would be delivered free to all households. It was radical; unheard of. He talked to local businesses, selling the idea that if they purchased advertisements in the paper, their message would go to every household. Several businesses pledged to purchase ads for the first four weeks of *The Camrose Booster*'s publication.

Our family of two adults and by then four children didn't have extra money. Before the first issue ever came out, the new business had start-up expenses for supplies and equipment and printing and delivery. It would be weeks before the first income arrived in the form of payments for advertisements.

Dad went to banks to get financing for the new venture. He showed them the advertiser pledges and his cash flow projections. No matter how enthusiastic he or the advertisers were, banks weren't impressed. They needed more security before they would consider any form of financing.

Eventually one bank agreed to provide a line of credit. The security for the line of credit was a percentage of receivables, the amount of money advertisers owed the *Booster* at any given time. For the first few years, the *Booster* generated enough revenue to cover expenses – barely – but the money always arrived after expenses had to be paid. That line of credit was the lifeline to keep operating.

~~~~~

Before the *Booster* was launched, my parents had ended a farming business partnership with my grandparents. That ending had created a large tax bill. (Mom said, "We were young and naïve and didn't know to plan for that.")

All their money was plowed into the fledgling business. At any given moment, the money people owed the *Booster* might be greater than the expenses, but the cash was not in hand.

My parents simply did not have the cash to pay the tax bill.

Dad went to Edmonton to speak with a federal tax official, explain the situation and offer a payment plan.

As Dad told the story, when he explained why he couldn't pay the tax bill in full right then, the tax person leaned back in his chair and said, "Frankly Mr. Fowler, I couldn't care less."

Dad reported that he was so angry he had to stomp around the streets of Edmonton for a while before it was safe for him to drive back to Camrose.

Dad left the tax official with post-dated cheques to cover the tax bill, but went away feeling uneasy.

A few weeks later on a Friday, Dad went on his regular sales calls, selling ads to local businesses. At his first stop, the business owner asked Dad about a letter the business had received from the federal tax department. The letter stated that if the business owed money to the *Camrose Booster*, they should not pay the *Booster* but instead should send the money directly to the tax department.

Dad was stunned.

It got worse.

In his next few calls, Dad learned that <u>all</u> the *Booster's* customers – all the advertisers – had received the same letter from the federal tax department.

The tax letters meant the *Booster* had no receivables and therefore no line of credit on which to operate.

As Mom said, "We were done."

That was Black Friday.

~~~~~

Sometime later, Dad got a phone call from one of the business owners asking him to come downtown to the store. When Dad arrived, a cluster of business owners and managers – all *Booster* advertisers – were there.

"We're going to the bank."

The group walked down Main Street to the bank. In the bank manager's office, they said something like, "We understand Bill has a problem with the tax department. We would like you to loan him the money to pay the tax bill. Just tell us how many signatures you need to cover the loan and we'll sign."

~~~~~

I did not hear this story until I was an adult. My stoic mom said that when Dad came home and told her what happened, it was the first time he'd ever seen her cry.

~~~~~

The name, *Camrose Booster*, reflects its purpose – to boost local businesses and boost the community. After Black Friday, my parents were even more passionate boosters of their community. More than sixty-five years later, the *Camrose Booster* is still proud to be The Home Town Paper.

When one door closes, another one opens.

~~~~~

Fast forward.

A few years after Dad died, Mom and I were at a symphony concert in Edmonton. It was during the time Edmonton was fundraising for The Winspear Centre – a new concert hall being built specifically for symphony concerts and other musical events. In contrast to all-purpose performance facilities, the Winspear Centre for Music was being designed and built specifically for optimum acoustics and whatever else would celebrate music.

The promotion material said, "Now there are three! The Vienna Opera House. The Sydney Opera House. And now, Edmonton's Winspear Centre."

"Hmp," Mom said. "There's only one that counts and that's the Vienna Opera House."

~~~~~

Every New Year's Day, Mom watched a TV special of the Vienna Philharmonic Orchestra's New Year's Day concert. She loved everything about it – the music of the Vienna Philharmonic, the dancers, the images of Vienna – and Walter Cronkite's hosting.

I got the germ of an idea. Wouldn't it be fabulous if Mom could be at the New Year's Concert in Vienna?

I ran the idea by my sister Beth. She lit up and began to do some research. We learned that tickets to the Vienna New Year's Day concert are sold out years in advance. But, we thought, we could visit Vienna in the spring time and go to some other concert in the Vienna Opera House.

(We learned that the Vienna New Year's Day concert is in the Golden Hall of the Musikverein, not the Vienna Opera House, but that didn't matter. We could attend events in both places.)

~~~~~

At one point I was fretting about how I would afford to pay my own expenses and half of Mom's. Beth was surprised I was thinking that. "We're not paying for her travel expenses," she said. "Why would we do that when her net worth is greater than ours? No, our gift is a ticket to an event at the Vienna Opera House!"

Right.

We created a pretend gift certificate that said, "This entitles Berdie Fowler to one ticket to an event at the Vienna Opera House" and gave it to her for her birthday.

~~~~~

Mom and Beth had both been to Europe, but it was my first trip. When the plane landed in Vienna, I was in love with the city before we left the airport. How could you not love a city whose airport bathrooms have marble counter tops and floors, and down-to-the-floor doors on the cubicles?

For us three classical music lovers, Vienna was heaven. On our first afternoon after the overnight flight, we hadn't planned any activities except a nap and perhaps a bit of a walk. While meandering around Stephanplatz, a square close to our hotel, we saw a poster for an organ concert that evening, right there in St. Stephen's Cathedral. We decided to attend.

So there we were, in the magnificent cathedral, hearing organ music composed by Johann Sebastian Bach, played on the enormous pipe organ that Bach himself had played...

~~~~~

That was the just the first of heavenly adventures in Vienna and Salzburg. We walked the streets where Bach, Beethoven and Mozart walked; heard Strauss waltzes in the dance hall where Strauss played; enjoyed an opera in a luxury box at the Vienna Opera House.

A music highlight was the concert in the Golden Hall of the Musikverein – where the New Year's Day Concert happens – with golden busts of famous composers who had conducted and played there. The highlight was a Mozart violin concerto, played so exquisitely that when the music ended, there was absolute silence for many seconds. Even the sophisticated Vienna audience didn't want to breathe. And then wild applause erupted.

Besides being immersed in music, we loved seeing the Lipizzaner Stallions and sitting in sidewalk cafes and enjoying Wiener schnitzel and Sacher Torte...

Mom kept saying, "Pinch me. Is this real?"

On the plane on the way home, Mom leaned over and said to me, "You know, I think you'd like to see London next."

~~~~~

A few months after we returned, Mom told me something that surprised me.

"When you girls gave me that pretend gift certificate of going to the Vienna Opera House," she said, "I thought it was so nice of you to think of it but I didn't really believe it would happen. And then the months went by and we made plans, but it didn't seem real."

She paused.

"Then we bought the plane tickets, but I still didn't believe we would really go. I just couldn't imagine it. I thought something would happen so we couldn't."

She paused again. "And then we were getting on the plane and I almost didn't believe we were doing that. Even on the plane it didn't seem real."

What she said next is something I will treasure for the rest of my life.

"You know," she said, "When your dad died, I thought I wouldn't have any more adventures. And now I think, maybe I could have some more adventures."

~~~~~

The next year we went to London.

When one door closes, another one opens.

Sometimes it just takes a while.

Work

On the Saturday morning of the day 93-year-old Mom had a minor stroke – which, as it turned out, was the beginning of the last few weeks of her life – she was writing her weekly column for the family paper, *The Camrose Booster*.

She hadn't quite finished her column but stopped because it was lunch time at the seniors' lodge where she lived.

She walked out her door and met the man across the hall coming out of his door. He said something funny, she tried to respond, and was horrified that instead of the words she was thinking, only garbled sounds came out of her mouth.

Telling the story later, she said, "I was so embarrassed. I basically fled back into my room."

She phoned my brother Blain and managed to communicate to him that something was wrong. He took her to the hospital where it was established that she was experiencing a minor stroke. It didn't seem like a big deal to her. By Sunday morning, she was ready to leave the hospital. However, later that afternoon she realized she was not fine after all and returned to the hospital.

Monday morning, Blain stopped to visit her on his way to work at the *Booster* office. He said, "It was not a hospital visit. It was a briefing session!" Her total focus was on what needed to happen at the office.

~~~~~

When mom was growing up, women worked – at home. The expectation was that women would be at home, looking after their husbands and children. That <u>was</u> women's work.

In later years, Mom told us that when she was growing up, women's place in the home wasn't demeaned, it was valued by women and by men. (Since then, I've been led to believe that looking after the household and children was an expectation of women, but their work may not have been universally valued.)

Mom had worked as a stenographer before she and Dad were married and for a short time afterwards. But for most of their first ten years of marriage, she carried out the traditional roles of caring for the home and children.

And then our family needed money. Dad's partnership with my grandpa had ended in acrimony. Then Dad found out that the real estate man he'd started working for was dishonest and cheating his customers. Dad quit and began the search for a new career.

That led to the launch of *The Camrose Booster* but it was years before the paper was financially stable.

With six mouths to feed, our family needed money and fast. Mom got a part time job at a local Variety Store.

It seems funny to me now, but I remember being horrified. As a ten-year-old, it seemed somehow shameful to me that our mother was going to work outside our home.

In those days, that's not what mothers did – at least not proper middle class mothers. I had only one friend whose mother worked outside her home (in the kitchen of a local café), and that was because my friend's dad was an alcoholic and didn't support the family.

In my ten-year-old mind, if our mother worked outside our home, that meant our family was in the same category as my friend's family – subject to the pity or disapproval of the community.

~~~~~

Looking back as an adult, I am still struck by the impossibility of what Mom and Dad did in the early days of *The Camrose Booster*. They were only in their early thirties, married for twelve years, had lived through the tumultuous war years, had four children and now were starting a completely new wild-eyed venture.

The idea of the *Booster* was radical. A free distribution paper that would be delivered to every household? Unheard of! One local businessman said, when he received the first issue, "A paper that you don't pay for. There's a business that won't last a year."

Other than Dad once being employed by the *Edmonton Journal* as a "road man" who travelled to rural communities to set up paper deliveries, neither Dad nor Mom had any experience in the newspaper business. No experience in any of the artwork or printing tasks (though Mom once drew an excellent pencil sketch of King George VI!). They had no experience in selling or in business finance. In fact, they had no relevant experience at all. Nada. Zip. Zilch.

If they'd been better informed, they might not have started. They were too ignorant to know it was impossible.

Looking back as an adult, I am also struck by the fact that my mother was not a risk taker – especially not a financial risk taker. But if launching a paper was what they were going to do, then that's what they were going to do.

Mom set up a card table in her and Dad's tiny bedroom. She would do the typing and artwork on metal plates, and she would do the bookkeeping. Dad would sell ads, somehow get financing, and in the early days, he drove the metal plates to a paper in a neighbouring community where the paper was printed. He also managed the carriers who delivered the papers.

Mom also continued to work at the Variety Store for a while, and of course she managed the household and looked after us four kids.

~~~~~

The paper expanded and moved into the basement – along with a printing press. Dad learned to run the offset press (a radical change from olden-days metal typesetting). The first staff person was hired to help with artwork, a part-time printer worked some evenings and a crew of "Tuesday Ladies" came to staple pages together on publication day.

Eventually the paper moved to commercial office space downtown and then to a building of its own.

During those years, Mom continued to work five and a half or six days a week (never on Sundays). As technology changed to electronic artwork and typesetting, she took courses and oversaw the changes in how pages were produced. She oversaw the transition from manual bookkeeping to electronic accounting. As the staff grew to about 30 people, she managed the editorial, artwork, reception and accounting departments.

Throughout those years, there was, I think, unrelenting financial pressure. It took a few decades for the paper find its financial footing.

During those years, in addition to the five and a half or six days of working every week, Mom also managed to find time to be involved in some community activities. I remember one evening I was visiting their home. Mom arrived home from a meeting about 10:00 p.m. She was full of energy as she came into the kitchen. "Now," she said, "What can I do next?"

My suggestion was, it being 10:00 p.m., perhaps she didn't need to work anymore that day. She gave me a puzzled look. It hadn't occurred to her to stop.

~~~~~

Once I mentioned that a friend of mine was upset because her husband worked all the time, seemingly day and night, and didn't spend much time with her or the children.

That made no sense at all to Mom.

"But that's how he loves his family," Mom said, "By working so hard for them."

It simply didn't occur to her that anyone might not understand that working is a form of expressing love for your family.

~~~~~

Work came first no matter what.

Sometimes some of us family members raised our eyebrows. When one of her out-of-town granddaughters made a special point of inviting Grandma to a milestone birthday party, Grandma said "yes" at first – and then declined because of something happening at the office.

In the days after Dad died, Mom didn't go to the office for a whole week, but it bothered her. It was statement week, a busy time for the accounting staff. "I know the girls can handle everything," Mom said, "But it doesn't feel right for me not to be there to help."

Mom tried not to show it, but it bothered her when the funeral of an extended family member conflicted with a busy day at the office. At another funeral, there was a problem at the office and she wanted some family members – including the son-in-law of the deceased – to leave the funeral reception and get back to the office to solve the problem. (Other family members intervened.)

~~~~~

I always thought nothing was more important to Mom than work – but I had a different realization when she was in her late sixties.

When Dad had major heart surgery 100 kilometers (60 miles) away in Edmonton, she was there at the hospital. When he came out of surgery and into Intensive Care, the hospital staff told her it would be many hours before she would be allowed to see him.

She decided to drive back to Camrose and work for a bit and then return to Edmonton.

When she returned, she was told that it would still be another several hours before she could see him. Again she returned to Camrose to work for a bit and then drove back to Edmonton.

Finally, the third time, she was allowed to see Dad. He was unconscious and hooked up to tubes and machines. She could see that his hands were swollen. She didn't know if the staff realized that his hands were swollen. "They don't know him," she thought, "So they might not know that's not normal for him."

What bothered her most was she didn't know if Dad knew she was there. The hospital staff told her it was time to leave and she drove back to Camrose.

The next morning she drove back to Edmonton and was relieved to see that Dad looked better and he knew she was there. She drove between Edmonton and work multiple times over the next many days.

When Mom told me the story about driving back and forth to work three times when Dad was in Intensive Care, I thought that was just another indicator that nothing was more important to her than work.

I was wrong.

Mom said, "It gave me something to do. That was less stressful than sitting in the Intensive Care waiting area with nothing to do but worry."

Oh. I got it.

Work was her salvation.

~~~~~

For years, Mom's sisters told her she was crazy to keep working long past the age when most people retired. Mom just smiled and nodded and kept working.

My siblings and I thought it was good for her. Even as her physical capacities diminished, her work kept her mind active and engaged with the world.

~~~~~

After another heart incident, Mom became physically frailer. The *Booster* set things up so that she could work on a computer from her home. They said it was fun to watch her computer at her office desk. They could see exactly what she was working on at home, proofreading or posting her weekly Pen Points column.

After she had the computer set-up at home, she still went to the office occasionally, but less and less often.

When the time came that she could no longer live on her own, she moved into a seniors' lodge where she had a 14 by 16 foot room.

When she moved into her room at the lodge, the most important thing to her was to make sure the computer was set up and working properly.

The granddaughter who was helping her move, asked, "Would you like me to go get some clothes from your home?"

"No," Mom said. "That can happen anytime. Setting up the computer is more important."

She was not satisfied until the technical people did all the tests (with cooperation from staff at the Booster office) and she was confident that the Booster/Lodge connections worked as they should. Not until she was assured she'd be able to work was she interested in anything else in her new living accommodation.

My son commented, "Grandma is probably not the only person in the lodge who has a computer. But I think she might be the only one who has a job."

From her room at the lodge, Mom continued to proofread, write her weekly column and provide input when new Booster staff members were hired.

~~~~~

In the last weeks of Mom's life, after she'd had a few mini strokes, she was diligent about doing everything she could to recover some of her brain functions.

She'd been told that physical exercise would help, so she – the woman who could never see the point of exercise – regularly walked up and down the hospital hallways with her walker.

"When nobody is around," she told me, "I sit in my chair and I practice thinking."

Mom was pleased that she could still remember all her computer passwords. That mattered a lot to her. That would allow her to work.

~~~~~

So. Mom's legacy of work.

My brother, sister and I are now all over seventy. All of us are still engaged in something we call "work" – though in my case, much less than I used to be and much less than either of my siblings.

A few years ago a friend asked me, "Have you ever thought of retiring?"

I said, truthfully, "It's never occurred to me" – though I did consider myself to be semi-retired.

She said, "Maybe you should think about it."

So I did.

Over the next year or two, I shut down most things that I called "work."

But this niggle won't go away. There are things I'd like to do in whatever time I have left.

This does not feel the way that "work" used to feel – as though I was not a valid person unless I was visibly working. This is something different, being pulled rather than pushed or pushing.

Perhaps work is my salvation too – but in a different way than it was for my mother. In my seventh decade, I'm learning new ways to be my own person – the person I am now, as "my own person" continues to emerge and change.

I don't know if that's what Mom experienced in the last years of her life. But it's where I've emerged – so far – from what I learned at my mother's knee and other joints.

I am profoundly grateful.

Coda

Postscript

In 2019, on July 1 (Mom's birthday), my sister Beth and her husband Jim drove home from Camrose to Calgary after our annual family gathering of four generations of Mom's descendants.

At the family gathering, Beth had received an earlier version of this book. As they drove, Beth read the manuscript out loud to Jim.

After all that driving and listening, Jim's comment was:

"She was not a normal woman."

There might have been other ways to say it, but he was right!

Berdie Fowler

She was born in a farmhouse in the East Bittern Lake district of Central Alberta on July 1, 1920, the firstborn child of Lilian and Lester Anderson. They named her Bertha Helen. They lived across the road from the farmhouse of Lilian's parents, George and Minnie Russell. A year and a bit later, sister Edna arrived, and about ten years after that, sister Doris.

July 1 is Canada Day. Every year the community held a giant picnic with games, races and even fireworks. Little Bertha thought the celebrations and fireworks were for her birthday.

She didn't start school until she was seven so that she and Edna could start school together. They rode on a pony to Ellswick School – a one-room schoolhouse with Grades One to Eight.

At ages 15 and 14, Bertha and Edna left home and moved into Camrose to go to high school. After high school, Bertha took a year of Business College at Camrose Lutheran College (now the Augustana Campus of University of Alberta).

During that Business College year, she and fellow student Bill Fowler became an item. She'd always disliked her first name and somewhere around this time, she began to call herself "Berdie."

Bill and Berdie were married in 1940. They lived in Edmonton where Bill was employed by *The Edmonton Journal*. Shortly afterward, because of the war in Europe, Bill enlisted in the Royal Canadian Air Force.

For a few years, Bill was posted to various points in Canada and Berdie was able to travel with him. Children Bonnie and Blain were born during those years. When Bill was posted overseas, Berdie and the children moved back to Camrose, living with her parents and youngest sister Doris.

When Bill returned after the war, they had a child, Brian, who lived only a few hours. Later, children Beth and Bruce were born.

After a time working at the Seed Growers plant, Bill formed a partnership with Berdie's father growing registered seed oats on two farms. The partnership dissolved, and Bill, Berdie and the children moved to a new home.

In 1952, Bill and Berdie founded *The Camrose Booster*, a weekly free-distribution paper. The paper became the centerpiece of their lives, with both Berdie and Bill working more than full time, along with being much involved in the community.

All four children were involved in the business, whether delivering papers, helping with stenography or artwork, working in the darkroom, running a printing press or selling ads.

On January 1, 1976, son Blain bought the paper. Bill retired and immersed himself in other community projects. Berdie continued as editor, proofreader, columnist and overseer of the art, accounting and reception departments.

In addition to her fulltime work at the *Booster*, Berdie found time to be involved in community activities such as helping to build Camrose's first school for children with developmental disabilities, helping to found the first children's day care centre in rural Alberta and being the first woman in Alberta and only the second woman in Canada to be President of a local Chamber of Commerce.

She was also involved with organizations such as Camrose Women's Shelter, Crime Stoppers and Business and Professional Women. Beyond the local community, she served on provincial bodies such as Alberta Opportunity Company and Alberta Apprenticeship Board.

For twenty-two years after Bill died, Berdie continued to be fully involved with the Booster and much involved in community organizations and events. She was a generous contributor to causes such as education, libraries, literacy, performing arts and – a special favourite because of its total-community perspective – Battle River Community Foundation.

Berdie was the matriarch of an ever-growing family. The original nucleus of two adults and four children grew to 47 people including five generations living on three continents.

She did her best to stay in touch with them, electronically and in person. She stayed on top of news and weather in Singapore and Brisbane where grandchildren and great grandchildren lived.

She enjoyed time with her children, grandchildren, great-grandchildren and two great great grandchildren and always had time to listen to children read or to attend their concerts, plays and soccer games. She especially enjoyed soccer games in which two great grandchildren who lived in different communities were playing. She cheered enthusiastically for both teams.

In her last decade, Berdie was recognized with a number of accolades and honours. When one of her great-grandchildren asked why she was receiving yet another award, she replied, "I think it's because I got old."

She continued to write her weekly column and help with *Booster* proofreading until a few short weeks before she died on September 24, 2013 at age 93.

Obituary of B. H. (Berdie) Fowler

With deep sadness we announce the death of B.H. (Berdie) Fowler, of Camrose, Alberta, on Tuesday, September 24, 2013, at the age of 93 years.

Co-founder of the Camrose Booster, along with her husband Bill, and a life-long champion of her community, Berdie lived a life based on service and gratitude. She worked hard for both business and not-for-profit causes that were of importance to her; she had high standards; and believed that if a job was worth doing, it was worth doing well. She often expressed how lucky she felt to be surrounded by the love and support of her many family and friends.

In her later years, Berdie was honoured to be inducted into the Alberta Order of Excellence, presented with a Queen's Diamond Jubilee Medal, a Canada 125 medal and an Alberta Centennial Medal in recognition of her many contributions to making the world a better place. In 2008 she also received an Honourary Doctorate of Laws from the University of Alberta Augustana Campus.

Berdie is survived by three children: Bonnie Hutchinson (Dick Chamney); Blain (Marlene) Fowler; and Beth (Jim) Balshaw; her sister Doris (Tom) Campbell; 10 grandchildren, 20 great grandchildren and 2 great-great-grandchildren, as well as many nieces, nephews, cousins and friends.

She was pre-deceased by her parents Lester and Lilian Anderson, her husband Wm. F. (Bill) Fowler, infant son Brian, son Bruce, sister Edna Francoeur and brother-in-law Louis Francoeur.

Berdie's four generations of descendants feel grateful and blessed to have shared so many quality years with their family matriarch.

Funeral services for Berdie took place at 2:00 p.m. on Saturday, September 28, 2013 at the University of Alberta Augustana Campus, Faith and Life Centre, 4901- 46 Avenue, Camrose, Alberta, with Rev. Brian Hunter officiating.

Thank you

Thanks first of all to my brother Blain and sister Beth for all the ways they have supported this project, and supported me over all these decades of being in the same family.

They were the first readers of the manuscript. I said, "If there's anything you don't want to be said, I'll take it out. If you see any errors, I'll correct them. If you have editorial suggestions, I'll consider them."

Neither of them asked for anything to be removed. Both of them corrected errors I'd missed and added details I'd forgotten. Naturally, as offspring of our mother, they both offered editorial suggestions – most of which I incorporated.

Blain and Beth have also ensured that all Mom's children, grandchildren, great and great great grandchildren receive a copy of this book, as will current members of the *Camrose Booster* team, many of whom worked with Mom.

Knowing that we choose our friends but not our relatives, I am grateful that my siblings and I, after all these years, actually like each other. As Mom said, "We just luck out!"

Thanks to Dr. Roger Epp and the University of Alberta Press for permission to include Roger's prose poem, "Doctor Fowler." It moved me to tears the first time I read it (while standing in a line-up to purchase his book!). In a few artful dignified words, he captured Mom's essence.

I've so appreciated conversations and email exchanges with people who knew Mom. I hope you enjoy "revisiting" her, and perhaps learn some things you didn't already know about her.

A happy surprise has been the many non-relatives who have been pleased to have this book about a woman they never knew. Thank you! Hope she enriches your life.

Thanks to Ian Kirkpatrick, the cover designer and artist, and to Budget Printing, for making production so easy.

Bonnie Hutchinson, 2019

About the author

After a career that included time as a graphic artist, teacher, community developer, executive director and government consultant, Bonnie Hutchinson launched an award-winning organizational consulting, training and research firm that served public and non-profit clients in four provinces and brought her joy for more than a quarter century.

Though she thinks of herself as semi-retired, most weekdays she's involved in something she calls "work."

For thirty years, whatever else was happening, she's been a spiritual explorer. For the past ten years, she's provided private energy/mentoring sessions that incorporate guided visualizations and meditations as well as more traditional coaching and consulting support. She also hosts free weekly "Just Send Light" online guided visualization sessions.

She writes a well-read weekly column for the *Camrose Booster*. Her previous book, *Transitions: Pathways to the Life and World Your Soul Desires*, receives consistent 5-star reviews on Amazon.

Among the joys of her life are two children, two children-in-law, four grandchildren, one grandson-in-law and two great grandchildren. She lives in Edmonton Alberta Canada.

Contact her at Bonnie@BonnieHutchinson.com